RI...
of
PASSAGE

MW01119482

Also by Elinor Lenz:

Once My Child, Now My Friend

The Feminization of America
(with Barbara Myerhoff)

RIGHTS
of
PASSAGE

*How Women Can Find
a New Freedom
in Their Midyears*

ELINOR LENZ

LOWELL HOUSE
Los Angeles

CONTEMPORARY BOOKS
Chicago

Library of Congress Cataloging-in-Publication Data

Lenz, Elinor.
    Rights of passage: how women can find a new freedom in their
midyears/Elinor Lenz.
        p.   cm.
    Includes bibliographical references and index.
    ISBN 1-56565-076-X
    I. Middle aged women—United States—Life skills guides.
I. Title.
HQ1059.5.U5L46   1991
305.4'084'4–dc20   91-4991
                                                             CIP

Copyright © 1992, 1993 by Elinor Lenz

All rights reserved. No part of this work may be reproduced or transmitted in any
form or by any means, electronic or mechanical, including photocopying and
recording, or by any information storage or retrieval system, except as may be
expressly permitted by the 1976 Copyright Act or in writing by the publisher.

Requests for such permissions should be addressed to:
Lowell House
2029 Century Park East, Suite 3290
Los Angeles, CA 90067

Publisher: Jack Artenstein
Vice-President/Editor-in-Chief: Janice Gallagher
Director of Publishing Services: Mary D. Aarons
Design: Susan Shankin

Manufactured in the United States of America
10 9 8 7 6 5 4 3 2

The author gratefully acknowledges permission to reprint from:

Breathing Lessons by Anne Tyler,
published by Random House, Inc., New York, N.Y.

Necessary Losses by Judith Viorst,
published by Simon and Schuster, New York, N.Y.

CONTENTS

૨૦

૨૦

RIGHTS
of
PASSAGE

CHAPTER ONE

Middle Age Is Not What It Used to Be

ONE

Since I turned 50, I have felt myself grounded on this planet. I feel more stable, integrated, self-sufficient. My vitality level is higher. I have given up trying to manipulate others. I have control over my life.

Pauline Watson, 50-year-old art teacher

I remember the precise moment when I was struck by the fear of growing old. It happened at my 50th birthday party when, surrounded by family and friends, I took a deep breath and blew out the candles on the sumptuous, three-tier cake. As glasses were raised in a toast, in this ambience of warmth and good feelings, I watched the flickering flames die out, and suddenly, I felt a chill. My mood, so upbeat a moment before, sagged.

Fifty! From here on, the future looked like a straight path with no detours to that dreaded end of the road: old age. It was not as though I had never thought about this before. All through my 40s, I had experienced a heightened awareness of the passing of time. I had tried to prepare myself for the day when my children, nearing adulthood, would leave, reminding myself that I was fortunate enough to have a solid marriage, good friends, good health, and many interests and personal resources. Why, then, was the idea of 50 so unsettling? Was this the famous, or perhaps more aptly, infamous midlife crisis?

I remembered coming across the words of a 50-year-old Bengali woman: "I am beginning to think that at the age of 50 something is wrong with life itself. We plan to be happy and do all sorts of things that our mothers and grandmothers and fathers taught us. I tried my best to be a good wife, a good daughter-in-law, and a good mother. I enjoyed doing it most of the time, but often I felt tired and did not see much point in anything. I found out, for example, that my son, no matter how much he loved me, would go away someday and love his wife. This is the way life is. But this knowledge could not make me accept it totally."

Is it possible, I wondered, that for women, aging is the great equalizer, cutting across class lines and cultural differences? Is it our age that gives us our identity?

WHO AM I IF I AM NO LONGER YOUNG?

To feel youth slipping away can be frightening, especially for women. From childhood, women have internalized the message that youth is a woman's most precious asset and when it is over, she becomes redundant. A woman's sense of herself, her deepest core of identity, has been firmly attached to her self-image as young and sexy. "Who am I if I am no longer young?" is a question that haunts many women as they face the prospect of becoming middle-aged.

The shock of recognition may take various forms. It may be a birthday, as it was for me. Or the death of a friend. Or suddenly seeing ourselves through the eyes of youth. "When I was 50," Simone de Beauvoir said, "it was a real shock for me to hear a young woman say to my face, 'You remind me of my mother.'"

Or it may be the birth of a grandchild. "My firstborn grandchild was what did it for me," confessed a 54-year-old department-store buyer. "When I looked at that tiny creature, I thought, 'She's going to call me Grandma.' My stomach turned over and I shivered. Grandma! I remembered my grandmother as a wrinkled, feeble old woman. I couldn't imagine myself in that role."

For another woman just turned 50, it happened when she was shopping with her mother. "My mother had left something behind on the counter and gone off to the next department to check out some sales items. As I started to follow her, the clerk called out to me that my friend had forgotten her package. I was startled. My mother was not quite 70 and had always looked young for her age. And of course, the clerk was a young man, so for him, all women past a certain age were lumped together. But still . . . it gave me a shock, I can tell you."

The day of reckoning may come when the traffic cop who pulls you over looks like your son. Or the ticket seller at the movies assumes you're eligible for the senior half-price rate. Or when, as a 51-year-old fashion designer tells it, "I couldn't see up close anymore. So I got those little half glasses. Then I looked in the mirror, and all of a sudden I felt much older. And I couldn't recognize myself. I couldn't find any connection between me and that woman staring back at me."

THE FACE IN THE MIRROR

One day you look in the mirror and you see someone who looks familiar and yet strange, a woman with pouches starting under the eyes, faint lines tracing a parenthesis around the mouth, the once-sleek body beginning to thicken around the waist. You wonder, Who is she? What does she have to do with me? You tell yourself that the mirror image doesn't reflect who you are, how you feel inside. Someone young, vibrant, sexually alive is hiding beneath that false image.

But another inner voice tells you this is for real and it is irreversible. What you are going through must be the midlife crisis, that much-discussed, much-analyzed trauma — the entry point to middle age. What will life be like from now on? Will it be downhill all the way? Or can life after 50 have meaning and purpose?

I thought of the women I knew, in my own comfortable middle-class world, who had arrived at or were close to their 50s. There was Esther, who at 53 became an alcoholic when her husband left her for a woman younger than their daughter. Esther, who had been raised in an orthodox Jewish family, had not suspected that her 30-year marriage was at risk, and the bitter and protracted divorce left her in a state of emotional disarray. And there was Helen, who sought relief from the pain of her son's drug-related death by joining a religious cult and was drifting off into a misty and incomprehensible world of her own.

But there were also women like Marjorie, who, in her 50s, started an organization to help unwed mothers. And Anna, who at 49, after the breakup of a love affair, started a catering service that has succeeded beyond all her expectations. And Lillian, who, after years of working at unsatisfying jobs, enrolled at a university for a graduate degree in education and is now administering a program to help displaced farm workers find new economic opportunities.

RESETTING THE CLOCK

Is there something that happens to women when we reach middle age, some convergence of physical, psychological, and emotional forces that propels us into a new orbit where we are infused with new energies but where there is also a danger of spinning out of control? Are we caught in a tug-of-war between our newfound freedom and our fear of aging? Is it here, at the midpoint of our lives, that we begin to feel that we are racing against the clock, that our lives are in a now-or-never crunch? Questions like these nagged at me, and as I searched for answers, I realized that one of the most revolutionary developments of the latter part of this century is the change in our experience of aging. We are facing the challenge of revising age-old perceptions of youth, middle age, and old age.

We can no longer be forced into rigid time slots. As recently as the 1970s, 40 was considered the starting point of middle age. At the beginning of this century, a woman was middle-aged in her mid-30s. A century earlier, Jane Austen "put on her cap" at 30, acknowledging that youth was behind her and she was no longer eligible for marriage.

As the life span is extended, thanks to the social, medical, and technological advances of recent decades, the midpoint has been pushed upward, and chronological age is no longer a reliable guide to where we are in the process of growing, changing, and aging. "You are young, and then you are middle-aged," Doris Lessing wrote in her book *The Summer Before the Dark*, "but it is hard to tell the moment of passage from one state to the next." Where is the map or compass, the guidebook or set of instructions that tells us when we are middle-aged?

In the past, the marker for women has been the menopause, when biology serves notice that the childbearing years are over. But for women today, the biological clock is no longer the only timekeeper. There are also cultural clocks, psychological clocks, developmental clocks, as well as any number of individual timepieces that are regulated by our genetic endowment and personal experience.

Today, women in their middle years can be as healthy and vigorous as they were in their early youth. Middle age is not what it used to be. But the middle age that is emerging is a new frontier in time with hazy boundaries and unlimited possibilities. Women who, because of their fear of aging and their biological clocks, have been more timebound than men, are beginning to explore this new life stage that is opening up for them. Along the way, they are shedding the myths and misinformation about middle age that they have been force-fed by a culture for which youth worship has been a form of religion.

THE NEW MIDDLE AGE

Until recently, middle age has had bad press. In Shakespeare's "seven ages," the age in the middle takes the form of "the justice, in fair round belly, with good capon lined," and with nothing to look forward to but the final stage: "second childishness and mere oblivion, sans teeth, sans eyes, sans taste, sans everything." Dante opens *The Divine Comedy* with these words: "Midway in the journey through life, I found myself lost in a dark wood strayed from the true path."

According to the traditional view of middle age, it is a time of decline and loss, especially for women. When marriage and motherhood were the sum total of a woman's life, middle age was a time when she became irrelevant. But there were some compensations. She could look forward to a quiet time, a voyage over calm waters. The cares and turbulence of youth were safely behind her. Her children were grown and living lives of their own. Her burdens and responsibilities were over, and she could now settle into a comfortable routine.

A more recent variation on the theme of the middle-aged woman depicts her as a pathetic figure, suffering from the empty-nest syndrome, overbearingly matriarchal (the Jewish mother type), struggling vainly to retain vestiges of her fading charms. In this version, she is lost and aimless. Her sexuality is a distant memory, her identity is fixed, and her choices have either narrowed or disappeared.

The new middle age bears little resemblance to either of these scenarios. In today's volatile world, the years between the 40s and the 60s are rarely a tranquil time for women. As a woman in her early 50s who is a marriage and family counselor sees it, "For women in their 50s, the idea of a single midlife crisis is a myth. Life at this stage consists of a series of crises—

sexual, psychological, marital, maternal, financial. This is the time when it all converges, when the strains, tensions, and conflicts collide. It's an emotional time bomb."

In fact, the midlife crisis, that much-discussed, endlessly analyzed trauma, is experienced very differently by the two sexes. In men, as studies have shown, the crisis tends to emanate from a single center: fear of the loss of sexual power (which has produced the familiar older man–younger woman syndrome). For women, the crisis is more complex. It is a balancing act involving an intricate interplay of biological and psychological forces.

A therapist I interviewed compared male and female sexuality to the difference between the solo instrument and the orchestra. "In the male, the sexual drive is concentrated on the individual performance," she said, "whereas in the female, it is diffused among a number of 'instruments'—emotional, psychological, physiological—which interact biologically." She also suggested that in middle age, men are at the peak of their careers and are ready to land, whereas women, now that their mothering years are behind them, are ready to take off. But, she warned, the takeoff is rarely a smooth, problem-free flight into the future, and women should be prepared for the bumps that lie ahead.

LOSSES AND GAINS

The middle years are a time of self-assessment, when satisfaction with what we have achieved is offset by regret at what we have failed to do. "If only I had known" and "Is this all there is?" are common feelings at this stage, and these compete with our feelings of pride and self-affirmation. Life often becomes a balance sheet with losses and crises on one side of the ledger, gains and satisfactions on the other.

On the debit side, a woman in midlife can expect any or several of the following changes:

❖ Family conflicts come to a head.

❖ The "sandwich generation" squeeze begins as aging parents who require special care are added to the responsibility of looking after still-dependent children.

❖ Career pressures mount.

❖ Money problems arise.

❖ Health problems arise.

❖ A parent dies.

❖ Her marriage breaks up.

❖ She becomes a widow.

❖ Her children turn into strangers.

❖ Time becomes an adversary to be fought off with diet, exercise, plastic surgery.

On the credit side, she can look forward to:

❖ A keener awareness of the preciousness of time, followed by the more satisfying use of it.

❖ The discovery of her authentic self following the casting off of the masks and pretensions of youth.

❖ The acceptance of what cannot be changed so that energies can be redirected toward realizable goals.

❖ A backlog of experience to serve as a base on which to make wiser decisions in the future.

Here is how a 55-year-old widow sums up the rewards she has gained after a long struggle with loneliness and self-pity: "I don't need the approval of others. I have created an environment that is pleasing to me. I no longer have to be 'on' all the time. I don't fritter away my energies on activities that have no meaning for me or give away pieces of my life to people who are marginal to my existence. I have time now for rest and contemplation. I can enjoy friendships with men. I have learned how to be alone without feeling empty."

The new middle age offers women opportunities to free themselves from the burdens and anxieties of their earlier years and live in harmony with their inner selves. But making a successful transition to this still undefined stage of life can be fraught with problems. Age cues inherited from the past are not easily discarded. Departing from familiar patterns of thought and behavior is rarely painless. Deeply held fears and stereotypes of aging persist and inhibit our growth.

But many women are overcoming these difficulties and are moving into middle age with renewed zest and confidence. New ideas about aging and new paths to personal and career development are revitalizing women's middle years. The traditional view of the middle-aged woman is being effectively demolished by women who are making remarkable strides in business, the professions, politics, the arts. These middle-aged women are achieving their goals while maintaining a delicate and often difficult balance between conflicting forces in their lives.

LIVING IN TWO AGES

Women who are in their middle years today are a generation in transition between two ages: the traditional age of their early youth, when women's lives followed a preset pattern, and the age that was ushered in by the women's movement and the social upheavals of the 1960s. Women of this generation have had to internalize two conflicting value systems. The traditional system was built on a historic division of roles and responsibilities between the sexes. Marriage was a lifetime commitment. Family links were strong and virtually indissoluble. Family and community took precedence over the individual. A woman's identity was relational: She was a daughter, a wife, a mother. Her life was centered on home and children;

her primary role was motherhood, and when that ended, she lost her focus and usefulness. When parents became old and could no longer take care of themselves, they were cared for by their children.

These values have been swept away in the rapid currents of social change during the past 30 years. Today, marriage is a temporary arrangement, "till life do us part." Mobility and the cult of individualism have replaced family and community. A woman finds her identity in her own development and in her achievements beyond the domestic realm. When parents become old and helpless, they do not depend on their children, who often live in other parts of the country or the world; instead, they move into retirement or nursing homes.

Women in midlife, straddling these two ages and juggling these two sets of conflicting values, often feel, as a 53-year-old financial manager described it, "like two different people living in one body." But history has shown that these intervals when past and future collide may contain "the moment of truth," as Hannah Arendt wrote in *Between Past and Future*. We do not have to remain mired in the past or be propelled unwillingly toward a future that is not of our making. At the midpoint of our lives, we are ideally positioned to use our past experience as a solid foundation for changing and growing in the present and future.

The middle years are a pivotal age for women, not an easy or problem-free time but a dynamic stage that offers new challenges and choices. As women learn to deal effectively with the conflicts and crises that arise during this midlife passage, they will discover that it can be the most invigorating and satisfying time of their lives.

CHAPTER TWO

ॐ

The Sandwich Generation: Caught in the Middle

ॐ

TWO

The acceptance of servitude has been handed down from mother to daughter for so many centuries that it is now a monstrous chain which fetters them.

Sibilla Aleramo, <u>A Woman</u>

Soon after I turned 50, I began to feel as though I was living in a pressure cooker that was steadily heating up. My parents, divorced and in their 80s, were in separate nursing homes, my mother recovering from a broken hip, my father incapacitated by a heart condition and near blindness. They looked to me, their only daughter, for comfort and support, and I accepted it as my responsibility to take care of them, as my mother had done for her parents.

Meanwhile, my teenage daughters were going through various forms of adolescent angst, which made communication between us an exercise in frustration. Shuttling between my parents and children and between anxiety and guilt made heavy demands on my time, energy, and patience. There was not enough of me left over for my husband, my friends, or my own needs and interests. Like so many women in their middle years, I accepted these pressures without question, assuming that they were as normal for this time of my life as the thickening of my waistline or the strands of gray hair.

The middle years are the age of the sandwich generation, when we find ourselves caught between still-dependent children and aging parents who require special care. In our longer-living society, it is no longer a rarity for people in their 50s and even 60s to be involved with parents and parents-in-law as well as their children and grandchildren. As a 58-year-old woman put it: "When I was growing up, I never expected that one day I would be a mother, daughter, and grandmother all at once."

Our standard script for women has placed family burdens disproportionately on their shoulders. If the script remains basically unchanged in the future, the average woman will spend 17 years caring for children — longer when, as in many families today, the children need emotional and financial support well into their 20s. As her maternal responsibilities are ending, she will begin caring for her aged parents and continue over a period of approximately 18 years.

The midlife squeeze was virtually unknown in the extended family of earlier times. When three generations lived together or side by side, the sandwich was a triple decker in which each level had its special value, and all three were interdependent. I grew up in such a family, and it gave me a sense of belonging, of a secure place in the scheme of things. This feeling is rare for children in today's precarious, split-level families.

The traditional family was not a utopia. It had its problems and shortcomings. It was a tight little island that discouraged independence of thought and action in its members. It was *interdependence* that gave it its strength and durability. The generations might have had their differences, there might have been little love between them, but they never questioned their dependence upon and responsibility for one another.

The most important function that the extended family served in its time was as a safety net for its members, especially for the tides of immigrants sweeping into this country in the early years of the century. At a time when government social services were minimal or nonexistent, the family support system served these "strangers in a strange land" as unemployment insurance, welfare, and social security. The tribe, the clan, took precedence over the individual.

The elderly had a respected place in this system, and when they needed care, they received it as their due within the family structure. My grandparents did not spend their later years in a retirement or nursing home. They lived and died in the home of their daughter, my mother, who was supported by the rest of the family in caring for them.

Today's nuclear family bears little resemblance to its ancestor. Its various shapes and sizes include the dual-income family; the single-parent family; and the stepfamily, also known as the blended or reconstituted family. It may consist of two working parents or a single parent, usually the mother, and various sets of children and stepchildren. At a recent bar mitzvah in Newton, Massachusetts, the rabbi introducing the members of the boy's family had to keep track of six pairs of parents and grandparents.

In this modern family, in which the traditions of kinship and community have given way to individualism, the emphasis is on self-fulfillment and self-esteem. The culture of narcissism, Christopher Lasch called it. Today's fragmented nuclear family has replaced interdependence with generational conflicts and tensions.

On one side of the sandwich is a younger generation, with its own values and culture, caught up in the fast-moving currents of a competitive, inflationary economy. From early childhood, they have been propelled along the slippery slope of upward mobility. "We're growing older younger" is how a 16-year-old girl expressed it. Education is extended; marriage and parenthood are placed on hold. Career decisions are given top priority and are approached with caution. All of which adds up to a prolonged dependence on parents.

Extending young adulthood into the 30s and even 40s is a way of balancing out the longer life span. The 30- or even 40-year-old who says, "I don't know what I want to be when I grow up" is simply recognizing that there is a long stretch of time ahead for being one thing or another — and it's not something to rush into. Better to take your time, and meanwhile Mom and Dad are there to provide emotional and financial support.

What about the other side of the sandwich, our aging parents? What is it like to grow old in our high-tech, youth-oriented world? In the past, when the elderly were integrated into the family and social system, they served an important function as custodians of the family history and mentors to the young.

Today's fast-moving, highly mobile society has replaced many of the informal connections between individuals and their family, friends, and neighbors with business and professional relationships. As a result, the elderly have become socially superfluous. In a consumer-oriented society, they neither produce nor consume in a significant way. The mass media have been slow in their response to the aging of the society. Except for laxatives and denture creams, advertisers beam their messages at the young. Films and television, with a few exceptions, focus on people under 40. Consigning the elderly to uselessness and marginality has been found to hasten their physical and mental decline and sap them of their independence. Today, poverty and illness are becoming less of a threat to the later years than loneliness and a sense of uselessness and dependency.

In the middle of this generational triple decker, attempting to hold it all together and make sense of it, are the midlifers. A generation in transition, they have integrated the values and behavior patterns of their growing-up years, when women's lives were shaped by traditional expectations, goals, and family pressures.

HOW DID I GET HERE FROM THERE?

So here you are in your prime, feeling fit and hip and sexy, your rough edges smoothed by experience, ready and eager to move on and make the most of these precious years. Why isn't it working out as you had hoped and planned? Until now, so much of your life has belonged to others — parents, husband, children, employers. Your needs, your interests, your aspirations have always been pushed aside. You've paid your dues and now it's your turn — to be free, to explore, to reach out, to give your life an exciting new spin.

Instead, you're trapped. "How did this happen to me?" is a question I hear again and again. I heard it from a 51-year-old woman whose father nicknamed her Skippy because she had skipped several grades in elementary school. Skippy is a tall, shapely woman, smooth-featured, her dark hair streaked with gray. I met her in an exercise class, and one evening she invited me to dinner at her house. Afterward, relaxing over coffee and brandy, she told me her story.

Two years ago, she walked away from a 25-year marriage. "It wasn't much of a marriage," she said, describing her ex-husband as "a self-indulgent man and a compulsive gambler. Why did I stay with it? There were the children, and family always came first with me — that's how it was with my parents. I didn't want to admit to myself or to them that my marriage was a failure.

"But it began to go from bad to worse when he went into his midlife crisis. I guess that's what it was. He was drinking heavily and having affairs with women half his age. I stuck it out as long as I could, until Josh — he's the younger one — left home for college. Now there wasn't any family to preserve.

"After the divorce I felt a tremendous surge of energy. It was the most incredible feeling, like being recharged. I enrolled in a paralegal program, got my certificate, and found a job with a firm of lawyers specializing in divorce and custody cases. I had an affair with one of the lawyers. It didn't last, but it made me feel sexually alive again, the way I used to feel in the early years of my marriage. My days were so full, they never seemed long enough. I loved my freedom, loved coming home in the evening, fixing dinner for myself or sometimes inviting friends to join me. I was never lonely.

"And then it all began coming apart. My 24-year-old daughter, Melanie, turned up at my door one evening. She'd broken up with Alan, her live-in boyfriend; she was pregnant; and she needed a place to stay while she figured out where to go from here. She wouldn't consider an abortion; it was against her principles. She was determined to make a life for herself and the baby. I told her to stay as long as necessary.

"Soon after that, my mother died of cancer, and I persuaded my father, who had retired several years ago, to move in with me. There was plenty of room in my house, and I couldn't bear the thought of him living alone, grieving for my mother. He resisted at first, but then he had a mild stroke, and when he recovered, he decided to take me up on my offer. It seemed only fair. He was always there for me when I needed him. Now he needed me. And reversing our roles like that made me feel good. Until then, I had always been the needy one.

"My father and Melanie didn't get along. They lived on two different wavelengths, and they kept rubbing each other the wrong way. My parents were very conservative, and among other things, Dad disapproved of Melanie's unwed motherhood to the extent that he showed no affection or interest in the baby. This grated on Melanie's nerves, and she was often rude and downright nasty to him.

"I'd come home from work looking forward to relaxing, and the tension in the air was like an electric charge. At one point I thought of suggesting that Dad move in with Arnold, my brother, at least for a time. But I decided against it. Arnie's life was unsettled; he was in the middle of a divorce and a job change; the timing wasn't right.

"Melanie wanted to look for work and get a place of her own, but I talked her out of it, told her she was needed at home to take care of the baby and help me with Dad, who was becoming more and more dependent on me. I could see she resented being put in that position, and she retaliated by spending her evenings at the local disco and running around with some unsavory characters.

"It was wearing me down, and I began having trouble sleeping. I made some stupid mistakes at work, and I was worried about holding on to my job. I kept asking myself, 'How did this happen to me?'"

And then, Skippy continued, there was a big turnaround in her life. She had reached a point of such desperation that she began to think about leaving—"just going off somewhere, alone, losing myself in a strange place. I could see Dad and Melanie calling the police, the newspaper headlines, my colleagues at work wondering, gossiping . . . One day I found myself driving around aimlessly in an unfamiliar neighborhood. A cop pulled me over and gave me a ticket. I'd gone through a stop sign and narrowly avoided a crash. At that point I knew that I had to pull myself together and do something before I went completely around the bend.

"I began seeing a therapist, a brilliant woman who helped me understand the damage I'd been doing to myself and my family. She made me aware of my double identity—my desire to live my own life, free of confining family ties, and at the same time my need to be needed, to have others dependent on

me. I'd been caught not only between two conflicting generations of my family but between two conflicting sides of myself.
And I was putting the same pressure on Melanie that I had put
on myself."

Now, two years later, Skippy is back to living alone and enjoying it. Her father has an apartment nearby and has regained
his former vigor and self-confidence. "He works as a volunteer
at the hospital, and he's taking an art class at the community
college. He looks 10 years younger than when he was living
with me," she told me when we met for lunch recently. "Melanie has a job as an executive secretary with an investment
counseling firm. While she's at work, her little boy, who's now
two-and-a-half years old, is at a day-care center. Melanie and
Dad visit me all the time, and it's amazing how much better
they relate to each other. I guess sometimes the family ties have
to be loosened so that you can get closer to each other."

LIFE ON THE DAUGHTER TRACK

Skippy's story, a classic case of today's intergenerational relations, has acquired the label of "the daughter track," a variation of the "mommy track," which has been blamed for putting
a cap on women's careers. We are entering an era in which
daughterhood is claiming equal time with motherhood as a
primary responsibility for midlife women. "Caring for a dependent adult has become, for many, a second full-time job," says
Bernard M. Kilbourn, a consultant with Caregivers Guidance
Systems, Inc.

When women's lives were centered on the home, it was assumed that caring for the family was their exclusive responsibility. It was one that women accepted silently, without question, says Louise Fradkin, cofounder of the support group
Children of Aging Parents (CAPS), which has more than
100 chapters nationwide. However, it was a relatively short-
term responsibility, mainly because the parents' lives rarely

extended beyond their children's middle age, whereas today, it is not unusual for elderly children to be taking care of elderly parents.

As demographics change and women become a major force in the workplace, the traditional family dynamics are no longer feasible. And yet, the old patterns persist. In the traditional family ethic, the adult sons in the family are exempted from parent care so that they can concentrate on their careers and on supporting their own families. A common complaint from women I talked to was that men felt caring for aging parents was women's business.

"We get letters from women who are taking care of their children and their parents and possibly *their* parents," reports Joan Kuriansky, executive director of the Older Woman's League (OWL). "They are running from place to place. How do we expect them to do that and stay employed?"

But we expect it of ourselves, as I learned from my own experience and those of many women like Skippy. The primal parent-daughter bond lies deep within our emotions. Our awareness of what is expected of us is like a sensitive antenna that is constantly picking up signals from our family and our community, signals that affirm our own feelings. Somehow we convince ourselves that we must do it all, make it all work, even if it takes superhuman strength and resilience.

IT TAKES THREE TO MAKE A SANDWICH

For women who feel they are being pressed out of shape by their position in the middle of the sandwich, a more realistic question than "How did this happen to me?" might be "How did I let this happen to me?" or even "How did I make this happen to me?" I arrived at this conclusion when my search into generational relationships revealed that many of us are co-conspirators in the process of becoming caught in the middle. It is a complex process, involving a web of conflicting emotions — love, pity, anger, guilt — which are intermingled with deeply inbred loyalties and obligations. Underneath, shoring up this shaky emotional structure, is the need to be needed, the primary source and basis of women's power throughout history.

Women in midlife have spent much of their impressionable youth in a time that regarded power as a dirty word when applied to the female of the human species. In men, power has been viewed as dispassionate, cool, rational, contained. In women, it has been seen as manipulative, dangerous, uncontrolled. In her book *Powers of the Weak*, Elizabeth Janeway described women as "the oldest, largest, most central group of human creatures in the wide category of the weak and the ruled."

The Power of Motherhood

The one area in which women have had power assigned to them unconditionally is motherhood. But even here, we have had to walk a tightrope between two common perceptions of the maternal role: the selflessly devoted mother and the dominating, "castrating" matriarch, the stereotypical Jewish mother. As for the childless woman, she has been considered as incomplete, a woman manqué, an object of pity.

When I compared notes with middle-aged women who have achieved positions of influence, they admitted that they felt less powerful in their present roles than when they were raising their children. My own experience was similar. Although my career as an adult educator has included the supervision of large staffs and the management of substantial budgets, none of this gave me the sense of personal power that I felt when my children were growing up and I was the center of their lives. It is not easy to relinquish that kind of power; for many women, it is so traumatic that they attempt to replicate it, often subconsciously, in all their intimate relationships.

Aided and abetted by today's extension of age boundaries, we become collaborators with our children in deferring their adulthood indefinitely. We agree that they should put off career decisions until they "find themselves." We encourage them to continue their studies, piling up degrees and credentials to equip them for the fierce competitive struggle that lies ahead. And since they may be in no hurry to enter that arena, they comply. "I stayed in school not because of a love of academic life," says author Ann Beattie, "or even because I wanted to buy time as a writer. I stayed in school because I didn't want to work."

During a discussion with a group of business and professional women whose ages ranged from the 40s to the 60s, one of the participants said, "I sold stocks to finance my son's education. I knew that when his schooling ended, I would have to face something I wasn't sure I was ready for: his independence.

"I felt torn. I wanted him to be able to take care of himself, but I also wanted him to go on needing me. He's on his own now. He's a junior partner in a law firm, and he's married to a nice girl. We have a good relationship, but of course it's not what it was when he depended on me."

Supporting Dependency

Many of us who were the first generation of affluent Americans raised our children on various forms of bribery. In the euphoria of having money, we rewarded good behavior with expensive gifts and punished misbehavior by withholding treats and goodies. Whether we were fully aware of it or not, we were using money to bond our children to us, hoping to shape their tastes and values in conformity with ours. And we have continued to subsidize them well into their adult years and even after they were married and with children of their own.

Here are a few extracts on this subject from my discussion with the business and professional women's group:

⁊⋆

"My 28-year-old son recently lost his job, and he's been borrowing money from me to pay his rent. I invited him to move in with me, but he refused. He says he'll pay me back as soon as he can, and in the meantime, he needs his own place. I don't want to do anything that might put a strain on our relationship, so I'm going to go on helping him as long as I can. But it's not easy. I'm also paying for my mother's physical therapy; she has arthritis in both legs and has difficulty walking. Sometimes at the office, when I'm in a meeting or talking to a client, I break out in a sweat from the effort to concentrate."

⁊⋆

"I persuaded my husband to lend our daughter the down payment for a house she wanted to buy. We don't expect her to repay the loan; she's an elementary school teacher, and her salary doesn't go very far. But I think at her age — she's 32 — she should own her own home. And if the time comes when we can't take care of ourselves and we have to move in with her, we'll feel better about it, knowing we helped pay for the house."

⁊⋆

"My 26-year-old daughter was divorced recently and she has custody of the children, three-year-old twin boys. She needs to become self-supporting; her ex-husband is an alcoholic and she gets no help from him. So I encouraged her to study for an MBA degree. I pay her school fees, which is OK. The problem is, I'm the baby-sitter for the children while she attends classes. She refuses to leave them with a sitter or at day care; she says at that age, children need the feeling of home and family.

"Since my husband died, I've been supporting myself as a commercial artist. I'm free-lance, I work at home — but it's impossible to get anything done when those two little demons are around. I love them dearly, but I worry about losing my main means of support. I can't let my daughter down, so I'm just going to have to manage somehow, even if it means working at night."

≈

"My son Jerry is 30, and he's been trying for years to make it as a writer. He's had a few things published, mostly in small magazines. I've been sending him a check every month, no strings attached, but recently, I decided it was time to treat him like a responsible adult. So I laid down some conditions. I had my lawyer draw up a loan contract, which set up a schedule for repayment. The next time Jerry asked for money, I handed him the contract. He signed it, but I could see he was angry about it.

"So what does he do? He goes to his father—we're divorced—and starts playing us against each other. Stan, my ex-husband, is a tightwad, but Jerry knows how to manipulate him. He couldn't resist Jerry's complaints about me, about how mean I was, refusing to help my own son when he was in dire need.

"Then it was back to me with a sad story about his father's stinginess and how if it weren't for me, et cetera. I fell for it and shelled out, never mind the contract. And so it went until I got suspicious and called Stan. When we realized how we'd been manipulated, we agreed—first time we ever agreed about anything—to sit down with Jerry and talk to him. It worked. Jerry has a job now selling real estate, and he pays his own rent."

≈

The need to be needed by our children is bred into us so deeply during their early years that, when they begin to show signs of independence, we feel as though a prop on which we have been securely resting is being taken from us. As much as we want our children to develop into autonomous human beings, we want them to continue needing us. In one way or another, we try to keep that need alive. But by supporting their dependency, we are maintaining the burdens and pressures that inhibit our own freedom to grow and change. We are missing the opportunity for self-enrichment at this promising time of our lives.

Parenting Our Parents

When we look at our relationships with our aging parents, it becomes apparent that despite the decline of the family the fifth commandment still has a strong hold on us. And here again, the problems are often self-induced. With the best of intentions, in honoring our father and mother, we encourage dependency in our parents. As in Skippy's case, we run the risk of becoming overprotective and assuming responsibilities for them that they may not wish to turn over to us. In my interviews, I came across several variations on this theme: "When my mother died, I thought I was doing my father a favor by taking over his grocery shopping for him — until I found out that going to the supermarket was one of the few activities he looked forward to. It got him out of the house, gave him something to do."

With our parents, as with our children, caretaking may contain elements of a power trip. A woman who describes her European-born father as "very authoritarian . . . his word was law around our house" admits that reversing the roles has its rewards. "Now that Dad is elderly and looks to me for advice and guidance on many things — like finances and problems with my mother, who suffers from depression — well, I've got to admit, I get a certain satisfaction out of telling him what I think he ought to do, laying down the law, you might say. It helps me work out some of the tensions that built up in me over the years."

We have many ways of making our aging parents feel helpless and dependent, often without being aware that we are doing so. In communicating with them, expressions such as the following, well-intentioned though they may be, tend to reinforce negative images of aging:

✤ You work too hard. At this time of your life you're entitled to relax and enjoy yourself.

✤ You really should give up playing tennis (hiking, partying, and so on).

✤ You shouldn't be living alone at your age. Why don't you find yourself a roommate?

✤ You ought to give up that big apartment (or house) and move to a retirement home. You'd meet other people of your age, and there'd be lots of activities you'd enjoy.

All statements beginning with "at your age" carry the message to our aging parents that they are crossing a border beyond which they must relinquish much of what has made life worth living for them. It is a message calculated to turn them into social dropouts and increase the likelihood of their becoming a burden on us. In our frequent telephone calls, we never fail to ask in a concerned voice whether they are feeling well and are getting enough rest and are taking their prescribed medications. All of our interactions with them suggest that we don't consider them capable of taking care of themselves.

This daughterly solicitude, however, may at times overlook the parent's deepest needs — for companionship, stimulation, self-affirmation. "My daughter calls me every day to find out if there's anything I need," a woman in her mid-70s told me. "She gave a dinner party recently. She works for a publisher, and her guests included the company's up-and-coming young writers. One of them is a favorite of mine. I read everything she writes, and I would have given anything for a chance to meet her. But when I mentioned it to my daughter, she said she didn't think it was a good idea. She thought I'd feel out of place with all those young people. I'm willing to bet it was she who thought I wouldn't fit in, that I'd embarrass her."

In talking to parents of women in midlife, I learned that their daughters were constantly urging them to give up the family home in favor of a retirement facility. An elegantly groomed woman of 50 reflected on her experience with her 80-year-old father, who, after the death of his wife, had gone on living alone in the large, rambling house where he had grown up and had raised his children. "I thought it was ridiculous for him to rattle around in that old barn of a place," the daughter said. "It had seven bedrooms, most of which he kept closed off. It cost a small fortune to heat, and it seemed such a lonely way to live."

Eventually she succeeded in persuading her father to sell the house and move into a residential community for the elderly. "It was a terrible mistake," she admitted, "and I've always regretted it. He was miserable there, and I think for the first time in his life he was really lonely. All those memories in the old house were company for him. 'Friendly ghosts' he used to call them. He became ill soon after the move, and I had to put him into a nursing home, where he died not long afterward. You can't imagine how many times I've wished I could go back and undo what I did. But at the time it seemed like the sensible thing to do. I took it as my responsibility to look after him according to what I thought best."

Our images of the elderly are in need of updating. Giant leaps in our knowledge and treatment of older people are making it possible for them not only to live longer but to remain healthy and active throughout their lives. Growing old today has its problems, as does every stage of life, but it is not necessarily synonymous with decline and helplessness. Today, more and more people in their retirement years are finding it possible to be as fully engaged with life as they were in their youth and to continue to preserve their independence.

BREAKING THE CYCLE OF DEPENDENCY

Women who have succeeded in releasing themselves from the dual pressures of the sandwich admit that it has not been easy.

There are no quick fixes or surefire strategies for dealing with the caught-in-the-middle problem. As with most life changes, the process takes time, patience, and a determination to stay with it. The goal is nothing less than the shoring up of our personal and family lives and the breaking of the cycle of dependency by making full use of the resources available to us, resources within ourselves and our communities.

We can begin by asking ourselves some hard questions about our intergenerational commitments.

The Younger Generation:

* ❖ How responsible am I for delaying their adulthood?

* ❖ Am I prolonging their dependency because of their needs or mine?

* ❖ Am I encouraging them to manage their own affairs effectively?

* ❖ Am I overemphasizing the goal of material success to the detriment of their creative and intellectual growth?

* ❖ Am I creating an environment in which they can develop and make full use of their abilities on behalf of others as well as themselves?

The Older Generation:

* ❖ Am I consulting my parents about decisions that affect them, or am I trying to run their lives?

* ❖ Am I in any way contributing to their sense of dependency?

* ❖ How much are they able to do for themselves?

* ❖ How much am I able to do for them?

* ❖ Are there others in the family who can share the caretaking responsibilities?

✦ Should I encourage them to move in with me, and if so, are our social environments and life-styles compatible?

✦ Are my caretaking activities based on guilt? A power trip?

✦ Am I providing more help than they actually need?

✦ Am I disrupting their familiar routines or needlessly denying them activities that give them pleasure?

✦ Am I making appropriate use of the resources that are available for their care?

Caretaking Services and Resources

When care is needed, a multiplicity of services, resources, and professional caretakers are available so that women can help their parents in a caring and responsible way without sacrificing their own lives. These are the types of caretaking services that are springing up in communities throughout the country:

Home Health Services: Professional caretakers who help the homebound. A home health aide assists with bathing, dressing, and other personal needs. A physical therapist helps in recovering from an illness or a physical injury. A visiting nurse monitors the person's condition and consults with the physician.

Adult Day Care: Programs that provide adults with a variety of health and social services in a group setting. Designed for people who do not need the continuous care of a hospital or other institution and are able to leave their homes. The number of these centers in the U.S. has grown from a handful in the early 1970s to more than 2,100 today. Activities include lectures, movies, plays, music, and dance performances. For the physically fit, there are sports and exercise programs. Many provide transportation and hot meals, and some have medical personnel on their staff. Average cost: $35 a day.

Meals on Wheels: Hot meals delivered at home five days a week to people who are not able to cook for themselves.

Care-Management Services: The arranging and supervising of support services—housecleaning, food preparation, transportation, shopping—that enable the elderly to live independently. Especially useful as an alternative to a nursing home when aging parents live at a distance from their children. Care management can be costly and is rarely covered by private insurance. Medicare subsidizes it only as part of another service, such as physician services. Medicaid covers it only in a few cases, such as some states' nursing-home preadmission screening.

Emergency Response Systems: A security measure for an aging parent living alone. The person wears a radio transmitter, which is activated by pushing a button, sending a message to a local hospital or police station and an emergency contact.

Elder-Care Benefits: A small but growing number of companies are developing programs to help employees who are also caretakers. A recent study by the American Association of Retired Persons (AARP) uncovered a variety of workplace problems related to caretaking: absenteeism, tardiness, unscheduled time off, excessive use of the telephone. Another study found that employee caretakers, most of them midlife women, experience "frequent anxiety or depression." Southwestern Bell estimates that more than 15,000 employees, roughly one-quarter of its staff, now care for aging parents and relatives. The program operates through a nationwide computer network of consultation and referral agencies. These assist employees in managing problems ranging from finding in-home meal services for their parents to selecting a nursing home. Programs vary widely in scope and funding.

FREEDOM WITHOUT GUILT

The dependency of child upon parent and parent upon child is an integral part of the human condition and as basic to survival as food or sex. We are linked by our generational ties, which can be loving and nurturing or constricting and burdensome. As both youth and the later years are extended, the midlife woman has become the linchpin of the family. Her position in the center gives her the opportunity to foster and maintain strong, caring family connections between independent individuals.

To fulfill her various roles — as daughter, wife, mother, caretaker, breadwinner — she must draw upon inner reserves of strength and resourcefulness, qualities that can all too easily be depleted by the pressures of the generational sandwich. Meeting family responsibilities without being crushed by them is an attainable goal for middle-aged women who, at this time in their lives, have earned the right to enjoy freedom without guilt.

CHAPTER THREE

The Critical Void

THREE

That's what it comes down to in the end, willy-nilly! Just pruning and disposing. Why, you've been doing that all along, right? You start shucking off your children from the day you give birth.

Anne Tyler, <u>Breathing Lessons</u>

During the hectic, overpressured years of child rearing, there were moments when I longed for the day when my children would be on their own and I would be free. Free to do what? My thoughts didn't take me that far. What I was feeling was a vague yearning for time that was all my own, time to explore and experiment, time to find the *me* that was buried somewhere beneath the pressures and demands of motherhood.

Mixed in with these feelings was a heavy dose of guilt. Was I an unnatural mother? Weren't these supposed to be the best years of my life? The years of fruition and fulfillment? I loved my children, deeply and devotedly. Was I failing them by harboring feelings like these?

And then there it was—the freedom I had longed for. In what seemed like a series of fast-forward frames, the children turned into adults, acquiring along the way their own ideas, jobs, attachments, possessions, homes. Their new lives took them thousands of miles away, reducing their vital, throbbing presences to voices over the telephone and occasional letters.

By this time, my parents were comfortably settled—my mother in an apartment she was sharing with her recently widowed sister, my father in a retirement home that offered the facilities he required, including lessons in braille. I was no longer sandwiched between two generations. I was free from the responsibilities and pressures that had weighed me down for so many years. Those two precious gifts, time and freedom, were now mine to use as I chose.

At last I had the opportunity I had been waiting for, the chance to concentrate on my own needs and goals. Now that it was here, why did time drag by? Why was there this gaping hole in my days? I busied myself with volunteer work, courses at the adult education center, and the occasional free-lance writing assignment. Eventually, the vacuum in my life was filled, but only after a difficult and sometimes painful process of adjustment.

THE EMPTY-NEST SYNDROME

Like many midlife mothers, I had accepted the prevalent belief of my generation that the empty-nest syndrome was an inevitable and unhappy by-product of the aging process. The image conjured up by those familiar syllables, "empty nest," is of a pitiful, aging woman bereft of all that made her life worth living. We have met this woman again and again in films, TV serials, and novels. She is Philip Roth's Sophie Portnoy, who is responsible for her son's infantilism, which expresses itself in his need to be sexually dominated by women. She is Mrs. Millstein in Woody Allen's *Oedipus Wrecks*. She is Momma in the Mell Lazarus cartoon. Motherhood is the source of her glory and her authority, and when it is over, she becomes a displaced person, struggling to maintain some control over the lives of her adult children.

Despite all the publicity this postmotherhood phase has received, we have few defenses to protect us when we arrive at it. Women in their 50s, who grew up in the postwar ambience of cozy domesticity, have been especially vulnerable to the doctrine of motherhood as woman's sacred calling. For this generation, the idealization of motherhood has been so pervasive that — whether they have been full-time or part-time mothers, with or without absorbing careers, supportive husbands, and myriad interests — the arrival of that moment when the youngest child leaves home catches many of them with their guard down.

IDEALIZING MOTHERHOOD

The idealization of motherhood has received fresh impetus in recent years from the mass media. We have seen the rise of the "new traditionalist" in the media, the "good mother" who has freely chosen full-time mothering, who is loving, tender, giving, patient, devoted, self-sacrificing. She derives her deepest satisfaction from spending her time with small children, subordinating her needs to theirs, finding her own harmony in the tempo and rhythm of their lives.

She brings to motherhood an innocence and a set of expectations that are untouched by the practical day-to-day realities of child raising. "There is a conspiracy of silence about what is involved in being a mother," says Eleanor Rolston, a marriage and family counselor. "It's as if we were afraid that, once women found out how much pain and anxiety and drudgery went into motherhood, they would stop having babies. So we paint motherhood in rosy colors and set it up as an ideal for women to aspire to."

In idealizing motherhood, we lay the groundwork for the empty-nest syndrome. The greater a woman's investment in motherhood, the emptier her life will seem when her children leave. Having defined herself first and foremost as a mother, she will feel stripped of her identity when this phase of her life is over. As she may have once asked herself, "Who am I if I am no longer young?," she will now be asking, "Who am I if I am no longer a mother?"

Since women have been given the primary responsibility for raising children, they are also held responsible for whatever goes wrong in their children's lives. Based on her experience as a clinical social worker, Janna Malamud Smith reports that "Mothers imagine irreparable consequences whenever they yell, stay late at a meeting, use the TV as a baby-sitter, forget to serve a vegetable, or leave a bad marriage." It is no wonder that motherhood is, for many women, an extended guilt trip that leaves them, when it is over, in a state of emotional confusion.

When I asked a group of women who had been full-time mothers what their feelings were when their children left home, these are the answers they gave:

❖ Lonely, distant from other people.

❖ Restless, impatient, short-tempered.

❖ Easily bored, irritable.

❖ Angry at things that wouldn't usually bother me.

❖ Vaguely uneasy without knowing why.

In a recent study, *The Motherhood Report*, Dr. Louis Genevie and Eva Margolies found that, though the empty-nest syndrome is not a long-term problem for most midlife women, many women do experience empty-nest feelings for a while. Some women felt ousted from their children's lives or as if they were suddenly out of a job. Others had difficulty allowing their children to lead their own lives. Those who were widowed or divorced suffered especially from loneliness. Here are some typical reactions to the early stages of the empty nest:

❧

"I have never been able to free myself from the feeling that maybe I could have done a better job. I can't accept the fact that I have done all I can and that this phase is over. It is hard to accept that you are no longer needed in a close, mothering way or that you are no longer involved in making the 'right' decisions for them."

~

"I was completely lost at first. I had to tell myself that he was really gone. His empty room depressed me."

~

"The hardest part for me was the feeling that I was no longer a primary focus in their lives. Being left out of their plans was very hard to take, even though I realized that was a natural thing. Watching them decide things you know are wrong for them, but knowing you can't really influence them anymore, is also tough. Over time I have had to learn to stand back and watch them learn and make their own mistakes without saying, 'I told you so.'"

~

"There was a big void in my life because all three of our children were married and left home for good within three months' time. The loneliness was almost unbearable. I had to remind myself that they were big boys now. I longed to hear their voices. It was hard to realize no one would be coming home to share events of the day."

~

COPING WITH CHANGE

For some empty nesters, this stage can be a time of marital crisis. The children may have been a source of conflict and dissension, but they also provided stimulation and diversion. Several women testified that their children had kept their marriages together and broadened their horizons. Once their children were gone, their lives narrowed, and they became a middle-aged couple entirely dependent on their own resources.

In some cases, with the shedding of parenting responsibilities, the husband and wife fall in love all over again. But if their personal resources are limited or if too much distance has developed between them during the child-rearing years, it may not be possible to maintain the marriage.

When adult children who have left home move back, as many are doing today mainly because of skyrocketing housing costs, the empty nest is not necessarily refilled. The children have developed their own lives and their own rules, and the parents find themselves living with a stranger who was once their little boy or little girl.

The parents' lives have also changed. They have become used to having privacy and time for themselves. Their energies are now centered on their own needs and interests. With the return of their grown children, they find themselves again taking on the parental responsibilities that they had put behind them. According to Marge Vinolus, a clinical social worker who specializes in the problems caused by what she calls boomerang children, "If the parents are unable to let go of their caretaking role or establish their relationship as a couple, the kid is going to come in and muck things up." Without a clear understanding on both sides, she warns, parents and children tend to revert to their former roles. The parents take care of housekeeping, meal preparation, and gardening, and they pick up the tab. The returning children slip back into a protected and dependent life-style.

Even a satisfying career does not always provide immunity against the empty-nest trauma. Today, many women with careers are marrying and starting families later than previous generations did, which means that they may experience the empty nest as a double loss. A woman who was the personnel director for a department store before her retirement told me what it was like for her. "I was married when I was close to 40 — it was my second marriage—and I was almost 43 when my son, David, was born. While he was growing up, we had a live-in housekeeper, and we sent him to the finest private schools. It was a good life, and I felt fortunate.

"When my husband died and David went off to college, I had some difficult times, but I loved my job, and my colleagues were my surrogate family. A year ago, I retired at the age of 65. David was living with me, and I was looking forward to spending time with him, doing things together that we hadn't been able to do when I was working. But a week or so after I retired, he told me he'd become a Zionist and he was going to Israel. He met a girl there, married her, and they're living on a kibbutz.

"I'm out of touch with most of my former colleagues. I guess that's par for the course when all you have in common is your work. I feel as though I've lost my surrogate family and my son. The two losses came so close together; maybe that's why it hit me so hard. It's been a rough time, very painful. I have some really bad days, when I feel like there's nothing worth living for. I think about how good I used to feel when I had my job and my family. I wonder if I'll ever feel like that again."

EMPTY-NEST PROFILES

Studies of motherhood by psychologists and sociologists have revealed certain patterns of behavior that increase women's susceptibility to the empty-nest syndrome. From these patterns, we can discern the outlines of three maternal models that are deterrents to a healthy mother-child relationship and to a pleasurable and gratifying postmotherhood stage. These are the supermother, the dutiful mother, and the ambitious mother. Though they are composites drawn in broad strokes and do not take account of individual variations, they can be useful as a guide to certain types of maternal behavior.

The Supermother

She is the woman who has dedicated herself to the single long-term goal of motherhood. Being a mother was her career, to which she brought her best efforts and a full-time commitment. The supermother presents an image of confidence in her maternal role that may, in fact, be a cover-up for a shaky sense of identity. Psychological testing of mothers and their children has revealed that supermothers are often insecure women who, as compensation for their feelings of inadequacy and insecurity, attempt to be perfect mothers creating perfect children. But they are actually responding to their own needs rather than to their children's needs.

When supermothers are confronted by the empty nest, they attempt to fill it with activities that at times take on a frantic nature. They join one organization after another and constantly attend meetings. They indulge in endless orgies of redecorating the house. They take courses in gourmet cooking, jewelry design, and art appreciation; have a fling with aerobics; volunteer for various worthy causes. They may or may not have genuine interest in these activities, but keeping busy to the point of exhaustion is an effective way to escape the vacancy they feel within themselves.

The supermother has a difficult time letting go of her children, and she continues in one way or another to manage her grown sons' and daughters' lives. In her novel *Breathing Lessons*, Anne Tyler has drawn a full-blown portrait of the manipulative mother in Maggie Moran, who schemes, lies, and uses every stratagem she can think of to keep her son, Jesse, within her maternal orbit. To this end, she attempts to patch up his marriage in the hope of regaining some of the control she once had over the lives of Jesse's ex-wife and their child. When all her busybodying efforts fail, she asks her husband, Ira, the classic empty-nest question: "What are we two going to live for, all the rest of our lives?"

For women like Maggie, the one bright promise that the future holds is the prospect of grandmothering. In a new generation, the supermother sees her opportunity for self-renewal in being able once again to take part in guiding and shaping a young life. She anticipates being more than merely an occasional baby-sitter. Her expectations are that when her children become parents, they will be in dual-income marriages and will therefore depend on her to perform as a full-time grandmother.

She is impatient for this day and is irked at her career-minded children's postponement of parenthood. "When are you going to make me a grandmother?" she asks them repeatedly. But when that hoped-for day arrives, she may discover, as so many women do, that even an adored grandchild does not fill the empty space in her life.

The Dutiful Mother

Although she loves her children and takes pride in them, motherhood as an occupation has been less than satisfying, a job to be performed out of a sense of duty rather than in fulfillment of a deep personal need. She has been a very conscientious mother, feeling that she must compensate for her lack of a strong maternal drive. Now, with more time and energy for herself than she has ever had before, she contemplates some of the sacrifices she has made for her children. A suppressed streak of narcissism surfaces as she sets out to redress those areas of her life in which she feels she has been cheated.

Reviewing what she now perceives resentfully as an unlived life, she sees her years of dutiful motherhood unfold before her as a series of might-have-beens. She might have been a famous actress, writer, or scientist, a successful business executive, or maybe even a doctor or a lawyer. She might have been irresistibly sexy, desired by rich and powerful men. She might have been able to travel the world and have exciting adventures.

Determined to make up for lost time, she begins by attempting to repair what the years have done to her face and body. She has her hair dyed and restyled, her face lifted, and her body reshaped with the aid of diet and liposuction. She becomes obsessed with clothes and fashion, choosing each addition to her wardrobe as if it were an extension of her evolving self.

Never quite satisfied with her self-creation, she feels the need to test her new, improved image in the sexual arena. She embarks on a succession of affairs, seeking from her bed partners the self-affirmation she needs even more than sexual satisfaction. But these catch-as-catch-can encounters rarely provide the ego support she is seeking.

If she is married, she tries to re-seduce her husband, who may have become an indifferent sex partner, caught up as he is in his work and, she sometimes suspects, in an affair with a woman in his office. She turns into a sexual manipulator, using all the seductive arts and crafts at her disposal, a strategy that may, in fact, revitalize her marriage, at least for a time.

But even if she succeeds in recharging her husband's sexual batteries, she finds that this does not compensate for all the might-have-beens in her life, nor does it overcome her dissatisfaction with herself or her fear of aging. In her effort to escape from the empty nest and make up for lost time, she may lose her sense of limits and become an alcoholic, foodaholic, workaholic, shopaholic.

The Ambitious Mother

She initially looked forward to the joys of motherhood without considering the responsibilities. If she has been a full-time mother, as she enters the empty-nest phase she feels frustrated, as if something has gone wrong with her life and she is not sure what it is. When she married and became pregnant, she had envisioned a close and loving family and a home that would be a haven of peace and security in which her children would find the inspiration and support to become outstanding achievers. If her own childhood was less than perfect, she expects to relive those early years in a more ideal way through her children. If her marriage is a letdown, her children are her compensation.

Her agenda for her children is clear: They will have the opportunities that were not available to her, and they will succeed where she has failed. From their achievements, she will gain a sense of self-worth that she has not been able to derive from her own experience. She pushes her children hard, impresses upon them the importance of good grades so that they can attend the kind of prestigious college that she is convinced is the doorway to a successful career.

Having built her mothering experience on the shaky ground of dreams and illusions, she is setting herself up for disappointment. "My children haven't turned out as I had hoped," she says. "I feel as though I have put a lot of work into them for nothing."

The ambitious mother who is herself a superachiever, whether she is single or in a two-career marriage, wants the very best for her children, and the very best is defined as a high level of achievement. Like other fast-track parents, her children attend top-ranked private schools where they are groomed to beat the competition. Despite the pressures of her career, she devotes every moment of her time at home to the children, moments that have come to be known as quality time.

She expects that her children will follow in her footsteps as superachievers, thus justifying the considerable time and money that have been invested in their future. It is when this expectation is not fulfilled that she feels the pangs of empty-nesthood. Her emotions are ambivalent: relief that she can now devote all her time and energy to her career, mixed with a sense of loss because of her children's failure to fulfill her hopes and ambitions for them.

REEVALUATING MOTHERHOOD

The three models of mothering outlined above are associated with the traditional image of motherhood as a woman's only source of identity and fulfillment. It is an image that is incompatible with today's social and economic realities — the high divorce rate, inflationary economy, and the growing number of women in the work force. And yet it continues to exert a magnetic pull on midlife women who are coping with the complexities and pressures of midlife and whose early memories are of a mother-centered home and family.

We are in a schizoid time in this postmotherhood stage. Much as we may wish to liberate our children and ourselves from the maternal yoke, it is not an easy or painless process. Emotions and behaviors developed during the years when they were small and helpless do not fall away overnight or without a struggle. We want to go on enjoying our children. We want the special intimacy of the mother-child bond to continue. The desire to help them, to keep them safe, to share their triumphs and ease their problems runs very deep within us. And most parents and children do not want to sever the connection. What we want is change *and* continuity. This, then, is the dual challenge that faces us when our mothering job is over: to reshape our lives around new goals and interests and to develop a new relationship with our grown, self-sufficient children that is free of domination and guilt.

In her book *A Woman*, Sibilla Aleramo asks, "Why do we idealize sacrifice in mothers? Who gave us this inhuman idea that mothers should negate their own wishes and desires? What if mothers refused to deny their womanhood and gave their children instead an example of a life lived according to the needs of self-respect?" Questions like these are being asked more insistently as women recognize the need for a new maternal model that is in tune with the realities of family life today.

As we reevaluate motherhood from a fresh perspective, we are beginning to strip away the idealization that has falsified the maternal role. The belief in a maternal instinct is fading as research reveals that mothering in the human species is learned behavior that some women learn better than others and that can be acquired by men. We are also discovering that the perfect mother is a false ideal which so distorts the maternal role that it is virtually impossible for us to find our fulfillment in it.

"We have proof that motherhood is not always the first and instinctive concern of the woman," writes sociologist Elisabeth Badinter in *The Myth of Motherhood*. "It is not self-evident that the interests of the child are put above those of the mother; that when women are freed from economic constraints and have personal ambitions, they do not always — far from it — choose to give up their interests, even for several years, for the good of the child."

Women's new attitudes toward motherhood are breaking through the "conspiracy of silence" that has perpetuated romanticized images of the maternal role. Most of the women surveyed in *The Motherhood Report* referred to earlier in this chapter felt that, although the good outweighed the bad, their positive feelings about motherhood did not negate the difficulty of the role.

Mothers with full-time jobs, whether single or married, are proving that children do not need full-time, obsessive maternal care in order to become normal, healthy adults. In fact, some psychologists maintain that full-time mothering is not necessarily an advantage for children and that children of working mothers are more self-sufficient and have a better chance of developing social skills.

Despite such assurances, working mothers tend to be more vulnerable to guilt feelings than homebound mothers, especially if their own mothers were full-time homemakers. These guilt feelings often resurface in the empty-nest stage, especially when the child's life takes a wrong turn, which evokes the self-blaming question, "Would it have happened if I had been there all the time?"

MOTHERHOOD WITHOUT GUILT

From the experience of women who have enjoyed being mothers and believe they have done a good job of it, we can develop a model of the guilt-free mother that looks like this:

❖ She has a realistic view of motherhood, and recognizing that the perfect mother is a myth, she keeps her maternal role in balance with other needs and interests.

❖ While loving and enjoying her children, she cherishes her own and her children's separateness.

❖ She knows that her children will leave her one day, but she accepts this as part of the natural ebb and flow of life.

❖ She encourages her children to find their own way, and she does not fall into the fatal trap of putting her own growth and development aside during the child-raising years.

MEETING THE CHALLENGE OF FREEDOM

An exhilarating feeling of freedom is the positive aspect of the empty nest that outweighs all others. "Wonderful, delicious freedom!" enthused a woman who had raised four children. "My husband and I feel as though we are newlyweds. We have time for ourselves. The house is quiet, peaceful. No more arguments about washing the dishes, picking up clothes, cleaning the bathroom, coming home at a reasonable hour. The telephone is available to us. We can watch what we want on TV. And we have extra money to spend as we like."

Asked about relationships with children, a 53-year-old woman who runs a small mail-order business from her home in Maine said, "My children and I enjoy each other now as we never did before. The tensions are gone. We're relaxed. We have fun together. I look forward to their visits. It's as if I've acquired two charming new friends."

Although we've seen how the critical void can disrupt a marriage, empty nesters who have made a positive response to the challenge of freedom report improvement in their marriages. These statements came from women whose children had left home within the past two years:

"My husband and I have more time for each other. We do things together we never had time for when the children were at home. We play golf, we go hiking, we travel. We entertain more. We're really enjoying our empty nest."

"Now that we're alone again, it's like we're rediscovering each other. He's more affectionate and more interested in what I think and how I spend my time. We're not as tired as we used to be. Our sex life is better."

"We can talk without being interrupted. We have more time and more money for ourselves."

THE PRICKINGS OF GUILT

Motherhood without guilt is the most effective immunity against the empty-nest syndrome. But can we rid ourselves of guilt when it has been so deeply embedded in the maternal role? It has been used by women as a weapon to control their children, and used against women to pin them to their mothering responsibilities. Beneath the most liberated feminine facade, the prickings of guilt need only the slightest stimulus to go into action and break through to the surface.

Women who have been finding a new freedom in their 50s offer the following prescriptions for healthy motherhood and a satisfying empty-nesthood:

❖ Be aware of your limitations. Being a mother does not give you the power to protect your children from all the problems and perils of life.

❖ Avoid unrealistic expectations of your children. This will guard you against guilt and self-blame if they don't turn out as you had hoped.

❖ Recognize that when your children are grown and able to take care of themselves, your job is done. There is no further need to offer them unsolicited advice or instructions on their behavior.

❖ If your children require financial or other help, treat their request as the basis for a transaction between equals. Should they move back to your home for a time, work out an agreement by which all concerned can live as equals.

❖ Reorganize your life around the goals and interests that are important to you.

❖ Do not devote so much time to your children that you neglect your husband. In a good marriage, both parents share in the upbringing of the children; when the children leave, the parents are each other's support system.

As women discover sources of power and fulfillment outside of motherhood, they can replace the feelings characteristic of the empty-nest syndrome with an upbeat response to the challenge of freedom. Some women describe it as a rebirth, the beginning of a less complex existence with new opportunities for personal growth and enrichment. For midlife women in the postmotherhood stage, there are unbounded possibilities for creativity and self-discovery. The empty nest can be filled to overflowing with the dreams and plans that had to be put on hold until this time.

CHAPTER FOUR

ﻖ

Marriage in Transition

ﻖ

FOUR

The majority of Americans still yearn for the comfort and satisfaction of marriage and family life, but they try harder than before to stretch the limits of these institutions to make them more receptive to enhanced freedom for individuals and less demanding of self-denial.

Daniel Yankelovich, <u>New Rules</u>

When I asked women in a midwestern support group, "What is the most critical change that has occurred in your lifetime?" the response was unanimous: marriage. These women, whose ages ranged from 45 to 60 and who had combined careers with marriage and motherhood, exemplified the extraordinary diversity of today's marital scene. The group included widows, divorcées — several had been divorced two or three times — women who had recently married for the first time, women who were in their second, third, or fourth marriages (one woman had remarried her former husband), women who were living with men to whom they were not married, women whose marriages were shaky, women in longtime marriages which they said were better than ever.

Marriage, once a stable and predictable institution, the rock on which society rested, is in transition, but where it is heading or what shape it may take is an open question. Women's social and economic dependence on their husbands, the stigma of divorce, the shame of spinsterhood, the repression of women's sexuality — these constricting forces, which once bound couples together indissolubly, have been eroding and are being replaced by new, flexible connections. Marriage and motherhood, once lifetime commitments, are now options, and women who choose to remain single and childless are no longer objects of pity.

Individual satisfaction and self-fulfillment are the twin pillars on which today's marriages are balanced. When those supports begin to weaken, the marriage is in danger of coming apart. Questions begin working their way to the surface: What happened to us? Do we still love each other, or are we just marking time? Is this what we had hoped for? Should we look somewhere else for the fun, the excitement we once had? If not now, when?

THE CRITICAL CROSSROADS

As we near midlife, signposts on the marital road carry a warning: "Approaching a critical crossroads. Proceed with caution."

Whether we call it the seven-year itch or the midlife crisis or dream up some other trendy label for it, marital tension usually appears when one or both partners begin to feel lost, neglected, misunderstood, unloved. Sex deteriorates, communication dries up, and blaming begins as they unload their disappointments and resentments upon each other.

Midlife is a time when unresolved developmental problems are exacerbated, when commitments come apart because one or both partners are clinging to expectations and self-images that were born in an earlier stage. Uneven growth patterns often open up a gap between those who have been married for many years, making it difficult for them to communicate in the open, empathetic way that was once so natural for them.

"People grow apart," says Jolene Dashut, a paralegal with the California Divorce Council, "and after 30 years or so of marriage, they sometimes become strangers. And they would rather live alone than with a stranger or someone they have come to dislike."

In longstanding marriages, the discovery by one or both partners that they are not on the same wavelength may be slow in coming. Or it may happen suddenly, as it did to a woman who until then could have been the model for She Who Has Everything. Elizabeth had a stable marriage, three bright, healthy children, and a successful career in advertising. As if that were not enough, she was also a talented artist whose paintings, on exhibition in a New York gallery, were praised by the critics as "bold" and "visionary."

But that was long ago, when she and Mark were living in a rundown studio in Greenwich Village and surviving on part-time jobs and subsidies from their families. Then they knew exactly what they wanted to do with their lives. She would paint and he would write. And they would dedicate themselves to making the world a better place.

Now, many years and three children later, they are parents, homeowners, solid citizens. They both have fast-track jobs, Elizabeth as the art director of an up-and-coming advertising agency, Mark as the sales manager of a large retail conglomerate. In the garage, a BMW and a Mercedes stand beside two bicycles and a power mower. They've made a good life for themselves and their children. What more could they want?

That question struck Elizabeth with full force when she was just past her 50th birthday. In a few weeks she and Mark would be celebrating their 25th wedding anniversary. A week earlier, their youngest child had gone off to college, but there was no room in Elizabeth's full and busy life for the empty-nest blues. She had her job; she was enjoying the peacefulness of their house in Connecticut; and at last she saw her chance to realize her long-deferred dream of returning to her painting.

One evening around nine o'clock, she turned off the television and went out to the terrace, where Mark was relaxing in his favorite reclining chair, puffing away at his pipe. She settled next to him, and for a few moments neither of them spoke. It was the kind of late-summer evening that casts a spell. A sliver of a moon hung in the blue-black, star-spattered sky. The distant hoot of an owl added a note of melancholy to the hushed silence.

Sitting quietly on their flagstone terrace and enjoying the peace of the evening, Elizabeth reached out and touched Mark's hand. She asked him softly, "What are you thinking about?"

He puffed on his pipe before answering. "I was thinking that if we cleaned up that room over the garage and put in a bathroom, we could rent it for a bundle."

Elizabeth withdrew her hand and examined her nail polish. After a moment she said, "But I was planning to use it as a studio for my painting."

He waved his hand impatiently. "When did you last do anything with your painting?"

"There hasn't been time, but now with the children gone — Mark, you know I've always wanted to get back to painting. I'm thinking of taking a leave from my job and —"

Mark sat upright and faced her. "Hey, this is the real world we're living in. We need extra income for the kids' college costs. The roof has to be repaired. There are the payments on the Mercedes. I'm not up for a salary increase for at least another year. And you want to take a leave from your job to paint pictures? Give me a break, Lizzie."

"Don't you ever think about anything but money?"

"Somebody in this family better think about it."

And so it went, their communication gap widening as they

wrangled over budgets and household economics and aired repressed resentments until the moon slid behind a cloud and it
was time to get some sleep if they were to have the energy to
cope with the demands of the next day.

THE COLLISION OF PAST
AND PRESENT

Elizabeth and Mark had arrived at that point in their marriage
where the collision of past and present forces us to measure the
people we have become and the lives we are leading against
who we were and what we had wanted out of life in our earlier
stages of development. This evaluation process, which typically takes place in the years between 50 and 60, is a necessary
part of our growth, the basis for making positive life changes.
But since change usually entails a move from the known to the
unknown, it carries a certain risk.

For Elizabeth, the awareness of risk was submerged beneath
the dissatisfaction that had been gnawing away at her ever
since that evening in the moonlight. She asked herself whether
she and Mark still loved each other or were just bound together
by financial and parental ties. She wanted more out of marriage, more out of life than just everyday maintenance. A standard of living wasn't the same as living. She was hungering for
the passion, the intimacy, the spontaneity of their early years
together. She wanted Mark to see her as a whole person, not
just as a wife, mother, and wage earner.

She began to pick away at Mark, and he retaliated. They knew
each other's vulnerabilities, and their fights, which were becoming more frequent, brought them close to the breaking
point. Anger was transforming their affection and trust, essential ingredients of a long-term marriage, into a festering
resentment.

But there was still much that bound them together, and before taking the drastic step of divorce, they decided to try a

cooling-off period. Elizabeth rented a studio in New York's Soho district and worked feverishly on a series of canvases expressing the sensibility of the aging woman. She sold a few paintings and was invited to submit her work to a major New York art gallery that was assembling an exhibit of women's art. But these achievements, satisfying though they were, did not assuage the aching emptiness inside her.

Mark was also attempting to cope with the trauma of separation. He took on more responsibility at work and had a brief affair with a woman in his office. But there were too many evenings sitting alone before the television set, too many empty whiskey bottles. Remembering those early years of their marriage, when he and Elizabeth were in tune with each other's every thought and feeling, when every moment was crammed with the sheer pleasure of being together, he wondered, Where did it all go? What happened to us?

Elizabeth and Mark are together again. They have simplified their lives, and their marriage appears to be working well. Elizabeth is finishing a painting that will be included in a major exhibit of contemporary art. Mark takes pride in her work and boasts about it to his colleagues. They were able to rework their marriage through a process of reevaluation that took time, patience, and a mutual determination to break through their communication barrier.

The process eventually brought them to an understanding of what had happened to them, of how their uneven development had placed them out of sync. Elizabeth was still trying to reconcile her need for commitment and connectedness with her creative drive, while Mark had already resolved that conflict. They realized that they needed to value their commonalities, manage their differences, and accept each other's weaknesses. And they agreed that in the future, they would control their anger, which nearly destroyed their marriage, by keeping their lines of communication open.

MANAGING ANGER

The long-established midlife marriage is especially in need of positive feelings to overcome the tensions and anxieties that are often stored away beneath the humdrum daily routine. This requires ongoing dialogue. The first and most important strategy for controlling anger and resolving differences is to keep talking. Take the time to sort out the feelings that brought on the outburst. Anger should be *managed*, not repressed.

Some guidelines for managing anger:

❖ Go below the surface to the underlying causes. Help each other locate the deeper hurts and wounds.

❖ Avoid insults, accusations, ultimatums, blaming.

❖ Resist the temptation to even the score. Nothing is as detrimental to a relationship as getting even.

❖ Listen with empathy. This involves putting one's own pain aside and focusing on the other's emotional state.

❖ Be forgiving. Love means being able to say you're sorry when you really are. It also means not repeating the anger-producing behavior.

❖ Consider the possibility of a developmental gap that with time and understanding can be narrowed. Adults continue to grow and change throughout their lives, and we need to accept these changes in each other as normal and healthy manifestations of the process of growing and maturing. Most important, we need to keep talking and listening.

WHAT SHALL WE TALK ABOUT?

"The children were the glue that kept us together" was what we heard from several women in the previous chapter. "They were our only topic of conversation." These women, who had been full-time homemakers, agreed that their domestic worlds and the business and professional worlds of their husbands had been so far removed from each other that they had little in common to talk about except their children.

But as we saw with Elizabeth and Mark, the two-career marriage is not necessarily proof against the communication gap. When both partners are in high-pressure, all-consuming jobs, there may not be enough time and energy left over for the thoughtful and sympathetic give-and-take that are basic to genuine communication. Tom Hayden has said in regard to the breakup of his 15-year marriage to Jane Fonda, "If Jane and I had an evening at home alone together, it was a scheduling mistake by the staff."

TILL LIFE DO US PART

The Hayden-Fonda split reflects a growing trend toward divorce after long-term marriages. The proportion of divorces among women between 55 and 59 and men in the 55-to-64 age group took a 10 percent jump in the 1980s. The reasons most often cited include longer life spans, dual careers, women's self-sufficiency, the older man–younger woman syndrome, the reduced stigma of divorce at any age, and in many cases, the self-knowledge and self-acceptance that comes with middle age.

At the root of our rising divorce rate in the middle and later years is our changing attitude toward marriage. In the not-so-distant past, marriage was considered a social institution that transcended personal needs and desires. Today, with our emphasis on individual fulfillment, "People are getting in touch with their own rights to happiness and freedom," says Carlfred B. Broderick, head of the University of Southern California's Department of Sociology. He adds that "It is remarkable that a person is willing to divorce when the chances for remarriage may not be that great. In general, people at any adult age prefer being married, but now the older ones aren't intimidated by any social requirement to have a spouse. You wouldn't have seen that 20 years ago."

Our relaxed attitude toward divorce is often blamed for the dissolution of some marriages that might have been worth saving. A woman who is active in the environmental movement said of her divorce 15 years ago that it may have been the easy way out, easier than trying to make the marriage work. She talked about it wistfully. "I was so insecure, so uncertain about who I was, what I wanted out of life. I was torn between wanting a man, marriage, children, and a career that was socially useful.

"Now that I am more secure about myself and what I want, I regret that I didn't feel this way in my 20s and 30s. I could have saved my marriage. I realize now how much I hurt my former husband and how I should have handled our relationship. When we fought, I should have been warm, affectionate. I should have been sexy. Instead, I was cold, I withdrew. It was because of my insecurity. Why does it take so long to grow up?"

However, she was quick to add that there have been some gains as well as losses. "I am having the most satisfying sexual relationship. There are no restraints, no fears between my lover and me. I don't expect him to satisfy all my needs. I don't confide my deepest feelings to him. I go to my women friends for that. What I want from him is his arm around me. Maybe that's what women should settle for — that arm around us. Maybe we expect too much of the men we marry."

Unreal expectations — in marriage as well as motherhood — are often responsible for the disintegration of midlife marriages. "The chief cause of divorce is disappointment," says Dr. Broderick. "If it was a long-term marriage, the disappointments are long-term, such as noncommunication, insensitivity, alcoholism. There is a new doctrine: I don't have to put up with this anymore."

A PASSPORT TO FREEDOM

To be able to say "I don't have to put up with this anymore" is the midlife woman's declaration of independence. It is only since women have been achieving economic self-sufficiency that they have been able to make such a declaration and act on it, even when it means walking out on a longstanding marriage. Today, a woman does not have to remain in a marriage that is painful and destructive. Divorce can be her long-awaited opportunity to become her own person.

But self-affirmation is sometimes a long, lonely, and painful process, especially when the marriage has been, as one 52-year-old woman describes it, a cocoon. "My husband was 10 years older than I and much more mature. He didn't want me to work or get involved in any financial matters, and that was fine with me. I liked being the child-wife, and he liked being the father-husband. In all the years of our marriage, I never paid a bill, made out a tax return, or had a clue about stuff like mutual funds and money markets."

One day at breakfast, with no prior warning, her husband announced that he was leaving her. His reason for dissolving their 30-year marriage was a textbook case of the male midlife crisis: He needed time to himself, to find out who he was and what he wanted to do with the rest of his life. With the children grown and gone, he felt he could concentrate on himself.

Now the child-wife had to grow up fast. "I went into shock for a while, but when I came out of it, I began to take responsibility for myself. I learned how to buy insurance, how to refinance my mortgage, how to handle my investments and my tax bills, how to talk in a businesslike way. It wasn't easy, but it's amazing what you can do when you have no choice.

"I have a job now — I'm a secretary in a law office, and I'm taking courses at night in a paralegal program. I should have my certificate by my next birthday. I feel a kind of strength inside that I didn't have when I was married. And I feel free; I have control over my life; I don't have to depend on someone else to take care of me. My divorce was my passport to freedom."

When I was in England last year, I met a woman who used the same words—"passport to freedom"—in describing her divorce when she was in her late 40s. She talked about it as we enjoyed a sumptuous tea in the living room of her cozy cottage in rural Somerset. She had been married for 28 years to a marine officer who took it for granted that she would devote herself completely to home and children and to entertaining his fellow marines. "I didn't fit into his world," she said. "I never felt comfortable with his macho military buddies. Toy boys, I used to call them. Toy soldiers playing their military games."

Before her marriage, she had been working in London as a ceramicist, and her pottery had been exhibited in several galleries and specialty stores. But her husband had no interest in her work. "He considered it rubbish, and he always referred to it as my 'hobby.' We never had any real communication. Whenever I tried to talk about anything personal, I could hear that drawbridge go up. I should have left him earlier, but there were the children. My daughter is 28; she's a ballerina with the Royal Ballet. My son is 23; he's a journalist. I stuck it out so that they could have the kind of lives they wanted.

"Now I can have the kind of life I want. When I told my husband I wanted to end the marriage, he said, 'You've changed completely.' But I hadn't changed. I'd gone back to being who I was 28 years ago. When I was married, I gave up my identity. I was living a life that had nothing to do with me. Since my divorce, I've come to terms with myself. I used to feel sluggish, only half alive. Now my energy level is up, and I have this feeling of stability, of being integrated, grounded on this planet. I'm working in ceramics again, and I'm teaching calligraphy in adult education, and I've set up a community crafts center. Am I ever lonely? Sometimes. But freedom always comes with a price tag, doesn't it?"

THE PRICE OF FREEDOM

For many midlife women, the price of divorce is a sharply re-duced standard of living. Alimony and child-support payments rarely cover the actual costs of maintaining a home and raising children in an inflationary economy. Women who have been full-time homemakers are especially hard hit by the need to find ways to supplement their income.

"It wasn't easy," says a woman I'll call Marta Lopez. When her 22-year marriage came to an end, she was forced to find a job for the first time in her life. "I couldn't support myself and two children still living at home on the $500 awarded by the court. But when I started looking for a job, my age and lack of experience worked against me. My family in Mexico helped me as much as they could until I finally found a job as a checker in a supermarket. I still have that job. I had to move to a cheaper apartment, and it takes a lot of scrimping and saving just to get by."

Another price tag attached to the midlife divorce is the effect on the children. According to Vern Bengston, director of the Gerontology Research Institute at the University of Southern California, the effect is usually divided between applause and dismay. "Kids usually are aware if their parents had a rocky and unsatisfactory marriage. The children's atti-tude sometimes is 'They weren't suited to each other. Why didn't they end it sooner?'" When the reaction is dismay, it is usually directed at the parent who initiated the divorce, espe-cially when the child had no warning or preparation for the breakup.

Since the children of midlife parents are likely to be grown and leading lives of their own, they are usually less affected by their parents' divorce than are the young children of earlier separations. Adult children, even when they are unhappy about the breakup of their parents' marriage, are spared the bitter battles that often rage around the custody of young children. In fact, as several women attested, adult sons and daughters often serve as the support system for their parents during the trauma of the divorce.

Whatever the price of freedom from an unworkable marriage, the majority of women I interviewed in this country and in England agreed that it was worth it. Sue Hubbell, who has written of her life as a beekeeper in the southern Missouri Ozarks, was shattered when her 30-year marriage ended. But when she came out of shock, she realized that there were gains that compensated for the losses. "If it leaves us no longer able to lose ourselves in the pleasures and closeness of pairing, well, we have gained ourselves. . . . We have time or at least the awareness of it, so we have learned to live as though we are mortal, making our decisions with care and thought because we will not be able to make them again."

IS LATER BETTER?

Is it this awareness of time and the thought and care given to important decisions that raise the odds in favor of marriages that take place in midlife? The answer would appear to be yes. In his comprehensive survey of *Love, Sex and Marriage Through the Ages*, Bernard Murstein suggests two factors that may account for the 75 to 80 percent success rate of remarriage: the experience, acquired in the first marriage, of living with someone else, and the effort to avoid those behaviors that brought on the first marital disaster. "There may be more involvement in protecting the marriage after one failure," Murstein comments.

The odds also favor first-time marriages that take place in maturity. In *Why Marriages Go Wrong*, James Bossard and Eleanor Stoker Ball note that "Early marriages do not permit the experimental contacts, the testing out of persons of the opposite sex, the utilization of courtship as a preparatory prelude to marriage."

When I talked with women in high-powered careers who had married for the first time in their 40s and 50s and who described their marriages as happy and secure, I was impressed by the way they had managed to combine romance with reality. I wondered whether they would have been able to do that if they had married at an earlier age. Certainly their views on marriage reflected a ripeness and seasoning that comes only with time and experience.

Speaking of their marital choices, they agreed that their midlife expectations were very different from those of their youth. "When I met my husband, I had stopped looking for Mr. Perfect," said a tall, pencil-slim corporate attorney who gave her age as "52 going on 25." She was married shortly before her 48th birthday, and she said, "It keeps getting better and better. My husband doesn't resemble in any way the dream man of my teens and 20s. He's not tall; in fact he's a few inches shorter than I am. And you couldn't call him handsome. And he's not very good at social repartee. And I earn more than he does. But he's loving, considerate, and always there for me. He gives me a nice, warm, secure feeling."

Marrying later has another advantage, which was pointed out by a petite, dark-haired university administrator who was married at 45. "You don't think about what you're missing. When you marry young, even if it's a good marriage, you can't help wondering now and then about the exciting possibilities you're losing out on that you could have had if you were single. But when you marry later on, you've had the career, you've had plenty of experience with men, you've traveled, you've been around, and you know there's nothing out there that's as good as this marriage."

But no relationship between two people can be entirely self-sustaining, and even a good, loving, mature marriage needs nurturing. There are certain basic requirements for maintaining the health and vitality of a marriage at any age:

❖ Having some private, unpressured time for relaxing with each other, for fun, for laughter, for love-making.

❖ Doing things together that both enjoy.

❖ Respecting each other's differences and encouraging each other to pursue separate interests and activities.

❖ Maintaining the freshness and spontaneity of the relationship.

❖ Staying in touch with one's own and each other's changing needs.

❖ Providing each other with support and empathy.

Midlife is a time when marriage is put to the ultimate test. Your parents die. The children leave. Friends move away. Now the two of you are dependent on each other as never before. As the external supports diminish, your marriage must be sustained by your internal resources, by what each of you has built up within yourself.

It's a risky time for marriage, these midlife years, a time when unresolved conflicts and confusions often come to a head. But it is also a time when the changing nature of marriage offers women in their middle years a new freedom — to marry when they are ready, to leave an unhappy marriage, to choose not to marry, and to seek in marriage a loving connection that is based on mutual understanding and empathy and a recognition of each other's right to be separate and equal.

è

Sexual Panic

è

FIVE

Our culture has tended to assign a kind of neuterdom to being over 50. And that couldn't be less correct . . . Sexuality is more than genitalia; it is more than orgasm and it is more than any other physical means of stimulation. It is by all means the total human being who is involved . . .

Ruth Weg, <u>Sexuality in the Later Years</u>

In my early 50s I gradually became aware of a subtle but unmistakable change in the atmosphere when I was in the company of men. Before, there had been a certain agreeable tension that I, like most women, had accepted as a natural manifestation of sexual chemistry. From the time we reach puberty, we take it for granted that being female and not outright repulsive is sufficient in itself to ignite a spark of sexual interest in the male animal. In my work, which brought me into contact with men of various ages and backgrounds, I had always been conscious of a tacit masculine acknowledgment of my femaleness that added its special flavor to the business at hand.

Now in my postmenopausal years, it seemed to me that the men I met professionally or socially reacted to me as though I were neuter, lacking in any specific sexual characteristics. They were friendly and pleasant but something was missing. I could have been "one of the boys." I wondered whether my imagination was working overtime. But when I compared notes with other women in their middle years — women who had never lacked for male attention and even those who were in secure marriages, as I was — I discovered that many of them were familiar with the experience of desexualization that I described.

There was considerable variation in the way these women reacted to the discovery of their neutered status. For some it was a relief, making them feel more relaxed, more comfortable with the men in their lives. "I'm happy about it," said one woman. "I'm not a sexy person. I never have been." Another woman said, "I never really enjoyed sex. I felt it was a duty rather than a pleasure. I had to do a lot of pretending."

But these were minority voices. More typical was the sense of loss, of "sexual panic," in the words of a woman who gave her occupation as "financial analyst" and her marital history as "a triple play — married and divorced three times." Just past her 46th birthday, she has the kind of vibrant attractiveness that is ageless and a bouncy energy that is a counterpoise to her self-deprecating humor. "Part of you becomes invisible. I knew it was all over when the guys in my office started including me in their typical locker-room talk about football and their recent sexual conquests."

Living alone in what she described as a "sexual desert," she is trying to come to terms with this feeling of being lost somewhere between two identities — the woman she used to be, for whom sex was her primary validation, and the woman she is becoming, who has not yet taken clear shape. She admits it is a struggle that is painful at times, but she is beginning to see a few glimmers of light just ahead. "No, not a man, though I'm hoping that will happen one day. But if it doesn't — well, I'm beginning to feel like a complete person all by myself, not just half of a couple. I'm even beginning to like and respect myself.

I never felt that way before, when I was in one of my miserable marriages or when there was no man in my life."

Women in long-term marriages were more ambivalent about their changing sexuality. Those in their postmotherhood years whose marriages had been sustained by more than physical sex felt at ease with their maturing bodies. "I was never a sex object, never wanted to be," said a woman who had been married for 30 years. "My husband and I are more relaxed now that the children are off on their own, and though we don't have sex as often, when we do, it's better than it ever was."

The anxiety that several women felt about the decline in their sexual appeal stemmed from their fear of that all-too-familiar domestic drama: aging husband leaves aging wife for younger woman. A woman whose roots were in rural Iowa confessed that a few years ago she had found out that her husband was having an affair with a waitress in the restaurant he managed. "She was not much older than our daughter, and though there were times when it hurt so bad I thought I couldn't bear it any longer, I kept it all inside. I figured it was that male midlife crisis you hear about and if I didn't rock the boat, he'd get over it. There was so much between us — our feelings for each other, our memories, the life we'd built together — I knew he wouldn't want to sacrifice all that any more than I would for a passing fancy." Eventually, she was proved right. The affair ended and the marriage went on as before.

Some women in long-lasting marriages were convinced that it was because of their declining sexual appeal that their sex lives had become routinized. "You know, every Saturday night after the 10 o'clock news" was the comment of a buxom, blond 50-year-old hairdresser. "But hey, I can't expect him to be turned on by my body after 20 years." She added that there was something to be said for predictability. "It's like going to church. I know what to expect and when to expect it, so I can put myself in the mood."

Becoming a grandmother can be a pivotal event that brings on an acute case of sexual panic. "For me, it was a schizoid experience," reminisces a 54-year-old widow who has established a successful market-research business. "I was deliriously happy when my granddaughter was born. I adore her and I enjoy every moment I spend with her. But being a grandmother — that hit me hard. It made me feel old and dried-up, like a sexual has-been. I was involved in an affair at the time — he was a grandfather but that didn't seem to have any effect on him sexually. Me, I couldn't handle it. I felt guilty, as though there was something shameful about my behavior, that it wasn't proper for a grandmother. I broke up the affair and haven't had another one since."

DOUBLE STANDARD, DOUBLE BIND

The sexual neutering of the middle-aged woman is a consequence of the imbalance in male-female aging. Men in their 50s, 60s, and even 70s can appear virile and sexy, whereas women are considered sexually obsolete by the time they reach their 50s. This lopsided view of aging has deep and stubborn roots in our history. In the literature of ancient Greece, Aristophanes' magistrate asks, "Don't the men grow old too?" to which that early feminist and peace activist Lysistrata responds that it is not the same thing, that when the soldier returns from the wars, even though he has white hair, he soon finds a young wife. But a woman has only one summer; if she does not make hay while the sun shines, she will afterward be left out in the cold, and she will spend her days consulting oracles that never send her a husband.

From our early teens, we are barraged with hidden and overt messages from the world around us that carry Lysistrata's dire warning: As females, our sexual timespan is short, so we had better make the most of our female resources before the dreaded deadline catches up with us. In *The Double Standard of Aging*, Susan Sontag describes aging for most women as "a gradual process of sexual disqualification. Since women are considered maximally eligible in early youth, after which their sexual value drops steadily, even young women feel themselves in a desperate race against the calendar."

The double standard puts single women in their middle years in a double bind: Men who would normally be their sex partners are attracted to younger women; men who are old enough to be available — elderly widowers, for example — are usually at the low ebb of their sexual powers. The race against the calendar becomes a frantic, last-ditch effort to halt the rush of time. But as long as women continue running in that race, even with the aid of dieting and dyeing and the latest advances in plastic surgery, they will be victims of sexual panic and will never know the meaning of true sexual freedom.

LIFE AFTER THE SEXUAL REVOLUTION

Today's middle-aged women experienced the rapid shift in values of the sexual revolution of the 1960s. Their lives have spanned an era in which changes in sexual attitudes and behaviors have been of epic proportions, amounting to a wholesale rejection of the past by younger generations. The women's movement, the Pill, and changing moral standards which include a new openness about sex have brought about a momentous upheaval in women's sexuality and in relations between men and women.

In the late 1940s, Kinsey's study of American sex lives revealed that 85 percent of men and 48 percent of women had slept with someone of the opposite sex before marriage. Of those women, more than half had confined their premarital sexual encounters to the man they eventually married. On college campuses, when students were asked whether they approved of premarital sex, 10 percent of both sexes responded affirmatively. By 1976, 75 percent of male and female students were sexually active. Today, many high school students regard sexual experience as part of getting to know someone of the opposite sex.

Over the last 40 years, our bodies have been progressively freed from social regulation. Not only have our sex lives become more varied, but we now talk about our sexuality more openly. We read in mass magazines about the roads to the multiorgasmic experience. The films we see offer up sexual scenes in an almost casual manner. The depiction of sex on the screen has become so frequent and varied that the regulatory categories seem unable to keep pace. Soft porn, hard porn, restricted, mature audiences — the regulations reflect the public's concern that some of the images on the screen may be disturbing to children. They would all have been considered smut by our grandparents.

Not only have men and women become more sexually experienced before marriage, but women have been discovering the geography of their own desire. Studies like those of Masters and Johnson informed women that they were as responsive to erotic stimuli and as orgasmic as men. The idea that women could derive as much pleasure from sex as men swept away the last remnants of Victorian repressiveness.

TWO SEXUAL PSYCHOLOGIES

And yet, sexuality continues to carry different meanings for men and women. Female sexuality remains closely connected to love, while male sexuality often operates autonomously, a carnal juggernaut kept in check by the bonds of marriage and societal convention. For women, the pleasures of intercourse lie as much in intimacy as in orgasm, whereas for men, sexuality is often a substitute for intimacy. Women are not interested in casual sex — this was confirmed by *The Hite Report* — because it does not satisfy their need for some sort of emotional involvement.

For men, sex is a performance, and every night is opening night, writes Barbara Gordon in her recent book *Jennifer Fever*. In this study of the older man–younger woman syndrome, Gordon points out that as men age, they dread the inevitable decline of their sexual performance, whereas women fear the loss of their fertility — the dreaded menopause — and all the losses of femininity associated with it.

Women's sexual insecurity has also been attributed to the difference in masculine and feminine acculturation. "For men of my generation, it's control and power rather than being able to enjoy another person sexually," said a 51-year-old woman who has been divorced for 15 years. "Men think of sex as a sport, with winners, losers, hits, runs, and grand slams. Women think of sex as an extension of friendship and intimacy."

She realized that it is only within the past year that she has been with a man who has satisfied her sexually. "When I was married and for years after my divorce, I lied about enjoying sex. I don't know any woman of my generation who hasn't lied about it many times. It was our conditioning. We grew up thinking we had to use sex to catch a man — it was a trap. And after that, we were supposed to please him, do whatever he wanted.

"The man I'm with now is special. He relates to me as one human being to another. He's not just going after his own pleasure. We share feelings and ideas, and we respect each other's moods. Maybe it's because he's younger than I am. Maybe these younger men who grew up with working mothers have a different attitude toward women. They're not attracted to bimbos. They want women who can take care of themselves. I see this as one of the really big changes in the way men and women are relating to each other."

THE CHANGING SEXUAL TRANSACTION

For centuries, the relationship between the sexes has involved a relatively simple tradeoff: sex in exchange for marriage and children. But with the widespread practice of premarital sex and birth control, that traditional transaction is no longer viable. Sex has been freed from the restrictions of marriage and childbearing, and today women can be as sexually liberated as men. But the question that confronts us is, Has this liberation brought about a dramatic improvement in the personal and sexual lives of men and women?

We see all around us a sexual landscape marked by disappointment, disillusionment, and a rising tide of violence against women. Never before has there been so much confusion and conflict between the sexes. One in every two marriages ends in divorce. More people are living alone. Loneliness is becoming endemic and is a frequent cause of depression and other emotional problems. The pattern of relationships between men and women shows a fast buildup to a passionate peak and an equally rapid slide into a pit of despair.

The sexual revolution has meant more sex, but for women it has not necessarily meant more satisfying sex. Permissiveness carried to an extreme can lead to repressiveness, or as Erica Jong put it, "The freedom to say yes to everyone and anyone is really another form of slavery." Jong, whose *Fear of Flying* was a landmark in the literature of the women's movement, expressed what many women have been discovering about the new sexual freedom: that meaningless promiscuity without commitment does not satisfy women's need for love and connection. Added to this is the fear of AIDS, which has made promiscuous sex too dangerous to risk. Clearly, the liberation of the body and the openness about sex have created as many problems as the solutions that this new sexual freedom promised.

ASKING THE QUESTIONS

"What's wrong with me? What am I doing wrong?" are questions that psychiatrists and family therapists hear over and over again from their women patients. More often than not, there is nothing wrong with these women. They are healthy, intelligent, loving, and physically attractive. Some have demanding careers. Others are full-time homemakers whose marriages are going sour. Their profile shows an age range from the mid-40s to the mid-60s and a wide diversity in family and educational backgrounds. In fact, about all they have in common is their desire for greater satisfaction in love, sex, and marriage.

When women cannot find satisfaction in their sexual lives, their responses may take the form of either rejecting men and marriage and becoming obsessed with work or projecting their fantasies onto any available man and having a relationship with the projection rather than the real man.

Neither of these responses can serve as more than a temporary distraction, as most women learn soon enough. But then, what is the course of action for today's normal, active, middle-aged woman who enjoys sex and wants emotional security together with sexual satisfaction? What does sexual freedom mean to women in these tumultuous times? "There are years that ask questions and years that answer," Zora Neale Hurston has written, and for women in midlife, these are the years of questions. In searching for answers, women are replacing ignorance and myths by some important truths about their sexuality. This process of sexual self-discovery is helping women lift the cloud of fear and insecurity about their sexuality that has hung over the midlife passage.

Can Women Enjoy Sex After Menopause?

One of the persistent myths about female sexuality is that women are prisoners of their hormones and that after menopause the decline in hormonal activity is accompanied by a drastic decrease in sexual desire and capacity. But in human sexual behavior, psychological factors are more important than biological factors. Unlike lower mammals, human beings are almost completely independent of the hormonal variations in their bodies. Women's sexual responsiveness is unaffected by the cessation of their menstrual periods and they can have a very satisfying sex life after menopause.

Is a Woman's Sexuality Affected by the Removal of Her Ovaries?

Women whose ovaries have been removed report some decline in sexual desire. However, if they have a warm, loving relationship with their sex partner, they can continue to enjoy sex and have pleasurable orgasms.

Does a Woman's Interest in Sex Change as She Grows Older?

In a recent survey of men and women over the age of 55, half of both men and women said their sexual satisfaction had not changed since their younger years. In various studies of sex in middle age and later, women have responded that sex improves with experience.

Are Women by Nature Sexually Passive?

In a male-dominated world, the idea of women as passive by nature and especially in their sexuality has been accepted as an unchallengeable fact of human existence. Sleeping Beauty is one of our most potent sexual symbols, representing the dormant female waiting to be awakened by the virile male. In the language of sex, the woman is object, the man is subject. She is "taken," "possessed," "penetrated," "fucked." Women who are active and aggressive in their careers and all other areas of their lives often turn into submissive sex kittens in bed.

Despite some changes in bedroom behavior since the sexual revolution, men continue to control the choreography of sexual intercourse. Responses of married couples in recent surveys indicate that in most cases, the man initiates sexual intercourse and determines the position, the rhythm, and the timing. Since there is a close relationship between sex and personal power — *potent* and *impotent* are key words in our sexual vocabulary — sexual passivity will probably not disappear entirely in women until they attain complete equality with men and full control over their lives. This applies particularly to middle-aged women whose sexual consciousness was shaped in the years before the women's movement. As British sociologist Mike Brake has said, "The more sexuality is brought into the open, into a 'liberated zone' freed from puritanism, the more women are open to exploitation by men unless they too contribute to the sexual debate."

Does a Career Make a Difference to a Woman's Sex Life?

More middle-aged women are working today than ever before, many of them in high-pressure jobs. Work and other responsibilities, such as dependent children and aging parents, compete with sex for time and energy. A German survey found that working women were too tired after work to be interested in sex. This finding is supported by research here in the United States which indicates that women who place a high value on their careers are likely to give a lower priority to sex than nonworking women.

However, there are some counteracting factors. In their book *Women in Midlife*, Grace Baruch and Jeanne Brooks-Gunn note that "exposure to the paid work world may promote the maintenance of social skills that are useful in the sexual marketplace . . . Additionally, the shared work world of men and women gives women access to a pool of potentially available sexual and marriage partners."

What Does It Mean When a Woman in a Longstanding Marriage Has an Affair?

When a woman sleeps with a man other than her husband, even if her marriage appears to be stable and secure, it means in most cases that her marriage is not emotionally satisfying to her. When a man has sex with a woman who is not his wife, it may have nothing to do with his satisfaction in his marriage. It is more likely that he is responding to a momentary physical urge or seeking to validate his virility in the sexual arena beyond the familiar boundaries of his marriage.

What Changes in the Years Ahead Are Most Likely to Influence the Sexual Behavior of Middle-aged Women?

Sociologists foresee four main changes in the sexuality of the next generation of middle-aged women: (1) Thanks to advances in health care and the extension of the life span, women will be accepted as sexual creatures throughout their lives; (2) Women will change sexual partners more frequently due to the lack of stable male sex partners; (3) Women will marry later after establishing themselves in careers, will continue working throughout marriage, and will be equal with men in sexual relations; (4) Women will have more extramarital affairs, not necessarily because of emotional dissatisfaction with their marriages but rather because they are seeking variety.

CHOICES AND CHALLENGES

Meanwhile, in the here and now of their middle years, women are facing an expanding array of sexual choices and challenges. The psychoanalyst Frieda Fromm-Reichmann has observed that for women the shock of aging is a "threshold shock. A door is closing behind us and we turn sorrowfully to watch it close and do not discover, until we are wrenched away, the one opening ahead." In the past, only two doors were open to women: either marriage or spinsterhood. Neither of these offered much in the way of warmth, intimacy, or sexual satisfaction. For the majority of premodern women, marriage meant continuous childbearing and drudgery. Spinsterhood represented rejection and failure.

Today, the middle-aged woman who is single and who wants a sexual relationship has so many doors open to her that her problem is finding the one that is right for her at this time of her life. Marriage or remarriage may not be a realistic option, since from middle age onward, the number of male partners available to her is sharply reduced by the shorter male life span and the tendency of older men to seek younger women as wives. But middle-aged women who want sexual relationships can consider the following alternatives.

Younger Men as Sex Partners

Reversing the older man–younger woman pairing is no longer confined to the fantasies of older women. As author Francine du Plessix Gray has observed, "The younger lover is becoming as fashionable among American women as jogging and homemade yogurt." As the taboos and constraints disappear into the past, it is no longer considered immoral or even unusual for a woman to choose as her lover a man young enough to be her son.

Why would a lusty young man be attracted to a middle-aged woman? Biologically, it makes good sense, since men reach their sexual peak at 18 and women in their 30s. But the pleasure principle is only part of it. Comfort, security, companionship, intellectual stimulation, and emotional nourishment are among the rewards cited by young men who are in sexual relationships with older women. Here are some extracts from a discussion with a group of male graduate students in their early to middle 20s: "I go for women who've had experience. They're looser, more relaxed, and you don't have to worry about getting them pregnant. They really appreciate you. They don't expect you to be dancing around them all the time. They don't lay their bad trips on you."

A few said they were attracted to women who were successful in their careers. "Money is sexy" was the unabashed comment of a 24-year-old Ph.D. candidate in economics. "It turns me on when a woman buys me presents. The woman I'm sleeping with now is a year older than my mother, but hey, my mother never drove a Subaru or bought me 60-dollar jeans."

However, bribery doesn't seem to enter into it in most of these younger men—older women affairs. The payoff for the young lovers is usually the sheer pleasure of sexual satisfaction with no strings attached. For the women, it is a wondrous and unexpected affirmation of their sexuality.

"I still can't believe this is happening to me" was the wonder-struck comment of a silver-blond, smooth-featured grandmother, a widow who, at the age of 53, is having an affair with a 25-year-old computer programmer. "He was my daughter's boyfriend. I was fond of him, and when she broke it off, he came to see me, just needed to talk, wanted a sympathetic ear. I'm still not sure how it happened but—I guess we had a few drinks and before we knew it, we were in bed.

"I wake up every morning thinking it must be something I dreamed, then I look at him lying beside me and I run my hands over his strong young body and we make love and it's beyond anything I've ever experienced before. My daughter thinks I've lost my marbles, but if I have, I hope they stay lost forever."

Crossing the Boundaries

Women are expanding and diversifying their sexual opportunities by crossing the boundaries that have traditionally narrowed their range of choice. As we become a multicultural society, and with the influx of women and minorities into the economic mainstream, men and women from various backgrounds are coming together as colleagues, friends, and lovers. They are erasing the once-rigid boundaries around religious and ethnic differences, physical impairment, age, education, and income levels. Also fading away are women's expectations of superior strength, achievement, and earning power in men. Today, Woody Allen is as sexy as Robert Redford.

Within recent years I have come across pairings of men and women, married and unmarried, who, when I was growing up, would not have had an opportunity to meet each other, let alone become sex partners. Their cultural profiles look like this: He was raised in New York in an orthodox Jewish family, she is a midwestern Episcopalian; he is a Chinese-American, raised in the Buddhist tradition, she is a southern WASP; he is a black American, brought up as a Baptist, she is American, of Sephardic Jewish origin; he is a Catholic whose parents migrated to Boston from Ireland, her heritage is orthodox Jewish with roots in Russia; he is Ethiopian Protestant, she is American Catholic.

In every case, both partners spoke of the rewards of crossing the boundaries: understanding of "otherness" and of the importance of sharing values which, they felt, enriched their humanness; acquiring greater tolerance and flexibility in dealing with people of various backgrounds, a valuable asset in our pluralistic society; developing the courage and openness to live with and find fulfillment in difference rather than sameness.

"Tell women not to overlook men with physical handicaps," advised a woman whose husband is paralyzed from the waist down. "I met him 12 years ago. He's a Vietnam veteran and is permanently confined to a wheelchair, but he can do almost everything an able-bodied man can do. We lived together for five years before we were married.

"My family and my friends had mixed feelings about our relationship, and sometimes, I must admit, so did I. I'm glad I didn't listen to them. We have a wonderful marriage and two beautiful children. My husband is the warmest, kindest, sexiest (yes, sexiest!) man in the world. Since our marriage, he has taught me more about courage, love, and values than most people learn in a lifetime. I focused on all the positive aspects of our relationship rather than the few minor inconveniences of living with a handicapped person."

Married Men as Sex Partners

For some women, an affair with a married man may serve as a compromise with today's social and sexual realities. With women outnumbering men in middle age and in the later years, and with men marrying younger women, the sex life of the middle-aged woman may consist of transitory relationships with married men who are available for extramarital sex, as long as it does not threaten their marriage. Women who settle for this option, however, must be prepared for sex without the intimacy or emotional security that is so important to female sexual pleasure.

The New Celibacy

Another alternative, sometimes referred to as the new celibacy, is being taken more seriously today, partly because of the fear of AIDS. Also, some middle-aged women are rejecting sex in response to the declining pool of available male partners and the problems that often accompany sexual relationships in today's shifting, unstable sexual environment.

Lowering the Threshold of Sexual Expectations

The treatment of sex in books, films, and other mass media has fostered in many women the kind of unrealistic expectations that inevitably lead to disappointment. When the experience does not meet their expectations, women often respond in one of two ways: by placing the burden of proof on the men and rejecting them for failing the test; or by blaming themselves for being sexually inadequate and withdrawing from the sexual arena. These women are victims of the Emma Bovary Syndrome. Emma thought of sex as "entering a marvelous realm where all would be passion, ecstasy, rapture . . . " When sex did not reach the soaring heights of her imagination, she was unable to cope with her despair. Developing a sense of proportion about sex and its role in a satisfying relationship is a prerequisite for expanding the sexual horizons of women in midlife.

WHAT DOES A WOMAN WANT?

When women today are confronted by Freud's famous question, their answers suggest that what women want in these fast-changing times may not be very different from what they have always wanted but have not been able to achieve until recent years. What women want in their personal lives is freedom of choice and self-realization. In their sexual relationships, they want a matrix in which sensuality and tenderness, friendship and commitment, independence and interdependence can merge and flourish. And despite the confusions and problems of this transitional age, these goals are being achieved by more and more women in their middle years as they shed the sexual myths and misinformation of the past and integrate their new freedom into their ripening sexuality.

CHAPTER SIX

You Have the Qualifications But —

S I X

With most married middle-class women, paid work — until very, very recently — was something that they shouldn't have to do. The women's movement, however, drastically altered this point of view so that, by the mid-1970s, every midlife woman I knew was making plans to try to reenter the job market.

Judith Viorst, <u>Necessary Losses</u>

"**S**eeking skilled writer experienced in working with press and TV for account executive position with leading public relations firm." The ad in the *Los Angeles Times* Jobs Offered section could have been written for me. There it is, my opportunity to reenter the world of steady employment now that I am free from the duties and responsibilities of motherhood. With two children in college, the extra income would be welcome, and a job in the fast-track world of PR is just what I need to absorb my energies and fill the empty space in my life.

I reread the ad several times. No question about it, I have the qualifications they are looking for. My résumé includes a job as account executive with a large New York public-relations firm where I had risen quickly in the company and was soon directing campaigns for several major corporate clients. My press releases and feature articles were being published in newspapers and magazines throughout the country. I was developing a reputation in the field as a whiz kid, and there was some talk about moving into a vice-presidency, the first time in the company's history that a woman would occupy a position at that level.

In time, marriage and motherhood took me into another world, and my husband's career took us to Los Angeles. In the intervals between homemaking, mothering, and entertaining my husband's clients, I wrote articles and occasional television scripts. But now I am ready and eager for a new challenge, for an opportunity to use my skills and experience in a demanding full-time job. I am nearing 50 and fit and free and raring to go.

A few days after the ad appears, I am sitting at a massive glass-topped desk in an office in midtown Los Angeles facing two middle-aged men, the president and personnel director of the company. I am wearing my best dress-for-success suit and the most confident, I've-got-what-it-takes expression I can manage. We ease into the interview with a few pleasantries and then get down to business. They tell me that I appear to have the qualifications for the job and they are especially impressed by my writing experience in both print and broadcast media. It also appears that being a woman is an advantage in this case since the clients who are to be represented are all in fashion, cosmetics, and similar female-related enterprises.

They ask me a few personal questions: Am I married, how many children do I have, what are their ages? I realize that this is their roundabout way of ferreting out my approximate age. We discuss salary and other job-related matters, and they bring the interview to an end by saying they will be in touch with me. A week later I receive a letter of regret: They are sorry; although I am well qualified for the job, they have decided on an applicant with more recent experience. I learn subsequently that they hired a woman in her 20s who had worked briefly in the publicity department of a film studio.

AGEISM AT WORK

My experience is becoming all too familiar now that so many midlife women are entering or reentering the job market. College costs, inflation, a reduced standard of living after divorce or widowhood, and other financial pressures are the main reasons for this phenomenal rise in the number of women in their middle years who, with the easing of their home-and-family responsibilities, are swelling the work force. But there are noneconomic reasons as well: the need for a personal identity after so many years of being immersed in the needs and growth of others and the desire for a sense of purpose and productivity. "Who am I if I do not have a paying job?" is another question that is central to our self-definition in a society that places a high value on the work ethic.

Here in the world of work is where midlife women feel most keenly the push and pull of living in two eras with conflicting values. Having been socialized to believe that child rearing was their primary and lifelong job, they are now in competition for jobs with younger women for whom a career is a lifetime commitment and who consider that marriage and children should not interfere with a woman's career anymore than they do with a man's. The result has been the emergence of a relatively new form of discrimination against women — ageism — which is subtler and more pervasive than the sexism of the past.

When today's middle-aged women were children, opportunities for women in the workplace were generally restricted to low-paying, low-status jobs. Women who had always worked, even while raising a family, were in a minority and were usually at the lower end of the economic scale. Since few midlife women with the educational background and capability for the more desirable, better-paying jobs were applying for these positions, age discrimination was not an issue. Today, it is very much an issue for women in their middle years who want to work.

Though men are certainly not immune to age discrimination on the job, it is more of a problem for women not only because of the double standard of aging but also because of the myths that are still associated with mature women. Middle-aged women are not reliable, one personnel director told me, because "they have these menopausal moods which affect their job performance." He went on to assure me that he does his best to be fair and even-handed, and he admitted that the company has some over-40 women on his staff who are doing a good job. But it was clear that age was a key factor in his evaluation of women applicants.

THE CHANGING WORK FORCE

Using age as a basis for hiring and firing was outlawed by the federal Age Discrimination in Employment Act of 1967, but though it has gone undercover, ageism is still alive and well in business and professional hiring practices. Personnel directors offer a grab bag of reasons for preferring youth in the executive suite: After 40, executives "pass their peak"; they become inflexible and resistant to new ideas and methods; the company's investment in them cannot pay off since their working span is limited; such company programs as group health insurance and pension plans are more expensive for older employees.

These arguments bear little resemblance to the realities of today's aging society. Studies have so far uncovered no evidence that after 40, executives pass their peak or become inflexible and resistant to new ideas and methods, or that older employees in nonexecutive positions are less productive than their juniors.

As for the higher-cost argument, many vocational and insurance experts maintain that employers who turn down productive talent because of pension costs are penny wise and pound foolish. Moreover, a pension plan is not necessarily more expensive in the case of the older employee. Many pension plans are merely deferred profit-sharing arrangements in which the employer makes yearly contributions that are limited according to various formulas by a percentage of the employer's profits and the employee's salary. In this type of arrangement, the employees' share of the fund does not become vested in them until after a fixed number of years of employment.

Even when the cost is higher for the mature employee, it is usually offset by the benefits, as some employers are discovering. Maturity can be an asset in most occupations, especially for women who have fewer stresses and distractions in their middle years and are able to invest themselves more fully in their work. The sense of personal security and self-understanding that many women arrive at in their middle years provides a firm base for their performance on the job. And their years of experience as family arbiter prove invaluable in their relations with coworkers.

Career counselors predict that in the years ahead, these advantages, which place midlife women on a career track that is right in line with emerging trends, will put an end to their problem with ageism. By the end of this century, according to a recent forecast of the Women's Bureau of the U.S. Department of Labor, America will have an aging work force with a high proportion of women and ethnic minorities. There will be a declining pool of youth. The shift to service industries will continue to rise. The demand will be for employees with high skills. A flexible, mediating approach will be necessary in dealing with a multicultural work force.

Women will make up more than 60 percent of the work force, and the majority of them will be between the ages of 35 and 54. The National Center for Education Statistics predicts that women will earn more than half of all degrees in medicine, law, dentistry, and theology. Today, nearly 18 percent of doctors are women, 22 percent are lawyers, 32 percent are computer systems analysts, and nearly 50 percent are accountants and auditors. With more women in their middle years entering the work force and with the aging of our society, we can safely predict that the prejudices against mature employees will be replaced by attitudes that reflect a more realistic view of maturity.

We are beginning to see some hopeful signs of an effort in business and the professions to adapt employment policies to the realities of today's work force. In 1990 a special issue of *Time* on working women reported that corporate efforts to diversify the work force are opening doors to midlife women, who are viewed as being steady and dependable and less likely to leave the job because of family pressures than younger women.

CONFRONTING THE AGE BARRIER

Despite these encouraging signs and portents, in this time of transition, women from their mid-40s into their 50s testify that job hunting still resembles a trek through an obstacle course, in which the most difficult hurdle to surmount is age discrimination. In times of normal economic growth, job seekers in the age range of 25 to 34 on average find a new job in 6.2 weeks; 10.5 weeks is the average for those 50 and older. "You have to work harder at finding a job when you're over 50 than you've ever worked before," says James Challenger, president of a Chicago-based outplacement firm. A comptroller in a Boston-based company told me that 10 years ago it took her a few weeks to land a job. When a recent merger eliminated her position, "This time, at age 52, it took over a year," she says, "and I had to settle for a lower salary. It was traumatic."

In some fields, the preference for youth has been rationalized in terms of specific business or professional requirements. The legal profession, for example, is biased in favor of young, recent graduates as clerks because, according to a senior partner in a large law firm, they are more "trainable." Until recent years engineering and the sciences were virtually off limits to those over 35. The basis for this rule of exclusion was the belief that the young are better able to keep up with rapid changes in science and technology. This has been exposed as a myth by the performance of older students in technical and scientific studies and by the work of such trailblazers as Rachel Carson and Barbara McClintock, who were in their middle years when they made their most important contributions to scientific research.

Women, young and not so young, are finding that they are less than welcome in the upper echelons of insurance, utilities, and banking, where promotions are based on seniority and status rather than merit. Professor Jeffrey Sonnenfeld of the Emory Business School calls these businesses "the Club," the fields where women, and especially midlife women, face the toughest glass ceiling, the old-boy bias that keeps them from rising to the top.

Film and television have also been exclusive preserves of the young. "I had to lie about my age to get the job I wanted," said a 50-year-old television executive who exudes youthful dynamism. "In the entertainment world, you're dead in the water after 40. Especially if you're a woman. Most of the guys at the top are in their 30s, and they've got the idea that movie and TV audiences are made in their image. So obviously, if you don't fit into that category, you're out of touch with the market."

What about the value of experience? "Forget it. I was in the business when some of these hot shots were just breaking out in adolescent acne. So then I take a few years off to do my home-and-mom number, and when I try to get back in, it's one turn-down after another. 'You're overqualified,' they tell me. Sure. The way they eyeball me when I tell them my age, I could be Grandma Moses. So what do I do? I take a good hard look at myself, and then I get my eyes done and a few little lines ironed out, and I go on a diet-and-exercise program. From then on, all I need to do is make a few changes in my wardrobe, my hair-style, and my résumé, learn the latest 30-something jargon — and before you know it, I'm doing lunch and taking meetings."

Should You Lie About Your Age?

Surely a lie about one's age in order to get a job is of the white, or at least the pale gray, variety. What's more, in our mobile, urban society, in which people invent and reinvent themselves, age is something that can be lied about successfully, even with-out the aid of plastic surgery, especially if it's a matter of just lopping off a few years. So why not deal with this problem by changing the figures to suit the requirements?

This question brings forth a surprising diversity of opinion from personnel experts. There are those who believe that lying about age is part of the game and justified in the rough-and-tumble competition for desirable jobs where the odds are in favor of youth. Another school of thought is opposed to lying under any conditions because it puts you constantly on your guard. Otherwise you might err in the manner of the 47-year-old assistant manager who claimed to be 36 and then requested a day off to attend the college graduation ceremonies of her younger daughter. Those opposed to lying about your age say it adds an element of risk to your job situation, whereas your objective in building a career should be to remove as many risks as possible.

The approach to job hunting in midlife recommended by most career guidance specialists emphasizes clarity about the kind of job you want; honest analysis of your skills and experi-ence; an assessment of what training you need in order to achieve your career goal; updated information about the occu-pations that are most accessible to mature employees; self-eval-uation with particular attention to the image you present to potential employers; developing an effective résumé; preparing for interviews; working with self-help groups that assist mature job seekers.

The Right Job at the Right Time

What kind of job do you want? This question is not as simple as it sounds, and it can present special problems for the middle-aged woman who has not resolved the contradictions between the values and aspirations of her youth and those of her maturity. If, for example, you are returning to the workplace after taking time out for child raising, you may find yourself in a job that was right for you in your younger years but doesn't fit the person you are today. We outgrow our jobs just as we outgrow our clothes, friends, and interests.

I discovered, almost by accident, that the job in public relations I thought I wanted would have dragged me back to the past instead of giving me a chance to grow and expand my skills and interests. A lucky chance in the form of a free-lance writing assignment led to an absorbing full-time career in adult education. It opened new doors for me and enriched the personal resources that I draw on in my writing.

According to psychologists and career counselors, more than 70 percent of people who work full-time are in the wrong jobs, or "misemployed." We can safely assume that women, especially those in their 40s and 50s, make up a substantial proportion of the 70 percent. Widows, divorcées, and single mothers, lacking a secure financial base, are often forced to settle for jobs at the level of survival. They do not have the luxury of choosing the right job at the right time.

A problem that besets many midlife women, especially those who have been full-time homemakers, is their tendency to devalue their skills and experience. "When I needed an office manager, I advertised for a homemaker," says Anne Salzman, a psychologist who specializes in career guidance. "Managing a home and family is very much like managing an office. Women who have been homemakers have done a difficult job, at times under great stress. They need to recognize the value of their experience." Salzman, who is a director of the Guidance Center in Santa Monica, confirms that when she interviews women who want to make the transition from full-time homemaking to a full-time job, the usual response to the question about their work experience is "I really can't do anything." Yet, during the process of self-evaluation that is a starting point in career counseling, the women often reveal abilities, interests, and accomplishments that are valuable as job qualifications.

Before you can determine what kind of job you want, ask yourself these questions: What do I enjoy doing? Do I have the skills and temperament for that type of job? What kind of training does the job call for? How much of my life do I want to devote to working? Am I willing to take on a job that involves a high level of stress? Do I have the resilience and energy to perform this job successfully? Is this job right for me at this time of my life? Can I grow in this job or will it be a dead end? From a practical standpoint, one question outweighs all the others: Where are the best opportunities today for midlife women?

THE BIG THREE

The influx of women into the workplace has accompanied the shift of the American economy from manufacturing to services. As we move into a postindustrial society in which production of goods takes second place to the care and improvement of human and natural resources, the special aptitudes and experience of mature women are becoming more relevant to the workplace. Even corporate executives, who have traditionally excluded women from their ranks, regardless of their age, are beginning to take notice of the feminine style of management—less rigid and hierarchical, more egalitarian and empathic—a style that comes with the ripening of women's experience and values. However, few women at any age have risen high enough to effect major changes in managerial behavior. And executive recruiting firms have nothing but negative information for middle-aged women who do not have strong résumés in corporate management.

For mature women the best opportunities are still in the traditional areas, the "big three": health, education, social welfare. These essential services, always considered as women's work, place less value on youth than on personality and experience. They have been growing and diversifying, a trend that is expected to continue in the years ahead.

Health Services: In health care, the emphasis will continue to be on rehabilitation and elder care. Nursing will remain at the top of the list for women, and there will be some upgrading in its scope and responsibility. An example of this trend is the nurse practitioner, actually a doctor's assistant, qualified to perform certain diagnostic tasks and examinations. She also makes house calls, filling an important gap between doctor and patient. The nurse practitioner is an R.N. who qualifies by taking an additional six-month course. She earns about 25 percent more than an R.N. The number of women doctors is growing, but because of the duration and expense of the training, few women enter medicine after the age of 40.

In recent years, the proliferation of knowledge in health care has led to increased specialization. You can now choose from a number of specialties, among them public health occupations that do not require a college degree, such as laboratory assistant, radiation-protection specialist, research analyst, health-program advisor. The aging of the society has created a demand for gerontologists, a specialty that is growing fast and that is wide open to midlife women, who have usually had experience in caring for aging parents. Gerontologists work in nursing homes, adult day-care centers, retirement homes, and hospitals. A college degree is not required, but it is necessary to have some training in the field. Universities are responding to the need by offering courses and degree programs in geriatrics and gerontology. UCLA offers a typical curriculum featuring courses such as "The Biology of Aging," "Social Aspects of Aging," "Health Aspects of Aging."

Advances in care of the physically and mentally handicapped are expanding the job opportunities for therapists. Specialties in this field include psychotherapist, physical therapist, recreational therapist, occupational therapist, speech and hearing therapist (also known as a speech pathologist or audiologist). Therapists are required to have a B.A. with a major in their chosen field and to complete a one-year course, usually in connection with a hospital program. There is also a steady demand for medical technologists, dietitians, pharmacists, dental hygienists.

A 50-year-old mother of three who became qualified as a dental hygienist three years ago reports, "I work under the supervision of a dentist, but I also work independently in my own office with my own patients, and I regulate the hours I work each week, as long as I put in the 20 hours I agreed on with the dentist." Flexible working arrangements and the fact that a college degree is not required make this an attractive field for women who are meshing a career with family responsibilities. According to current projections, there will be more jobs in the years ahead than hygienists to fill them. Several colleges and universities offer two-year training programs and degree programs for those who want to go into research or teaching.

Social Work: The need for qualified people in social work is growing rapidly as traditional values and institutions disintegrate, loneliness and alienation replace family and community, and drugs, poverty, homelessness, and violence spread alarmingly, particularly in large cities. Social workers assist individuals and families with their problems and put them in touch with the public services available to them.

Here again, the experience of midlife women who have raised families is the best possible background for a job in this field. Social workers are employed in public schools, community agencies, and hospitals, and psychiatric social workers in mental health centers and clinics. Recommended training: a bachelor's degree, preferably with a major in the social sciences, and a master's degree in social work. A specialty that combines therapy and social work is marriage and family counseling. Women in their 50s and even 60s are becoming licensed in this field and are finding that their mature expertise is an advantage in working with the marital and family problems of their clients.

Education: The outlook for the teaching profession is somewhat hazy. Jobs in elementary and secondary teaching have been declining because of the leveling off of the baby boom. However, the field is showing healthy growth in such areas as adult education, bilingual education, and special education. If you enjoy working with very young children, you can apply for a job at a day-care center or open one of your own; this seems to be the wave of the future. In all of these areas, your experience and maturity will be valuable assets on the job.

If education is your career choice, you can improve your chances by taking a broader view of the field. Today, there is more to education than teaching school. You might consider, for example, working as an editor for a textbook publisher, a researcher for an educational filmmaker, or an administrator in a company that produces educational materials. Or you might look into corporate training programs that have been set up to deal with the increasing heterogeneity of employees. Consultants as well as regular staffers are employed to develop and administer programs in "workplace literacy," the corporate phrase for improving employee competence in English. For this type of job, age is a less important factor than the requisite training.

WHERE AGE IS AN ADVANTAGE

Women who are looking for employment opportunities that require little or no training should consider working in sales. This is another occupation in which personality and ability outweigh the age factor. In fact, in some areas, such as real estate, the odds are in favor of maturity. "People who are making a major investment in a home or business property don't want to deal with a kid just out of school," says a realtor who has been in the business for more than 20 years. He says that in his company, the preference is for women over 40. "Home buyers feel more confident with a woman who looks like she's had some experience and knows something about a family's housing requirements."

Although many sales jobs pay low salaries in the beginning, a commission arrangement can give your income a sizable boost, and a good sales record in retailing can grow into a job as a buyer or merchandising executive.

NONTRADITIONAL CHOICES AND CHALLENGES

Many jobs that have been opening up for women in recent years are considered nontraditional because, until equal opportunity laws came into force, these occupations were closed off to women. Welding, tapering, riding in patrol cars, riveting, repairing television sets — not very long ago, women applying for jobs like these would have been greeted with derisive laughter. Today, women represent 38 percent of the industrial work force, and more than 25 percent of trade-union members are women. And since it was gender rather than age that was the barrier, these jobs are open to middle-aged women who have the training. And as many women are discovering, the rates of pay for jobs in the trades are higher than the salaries of many white-collar occupations.

If you want to work in a trade, you can begin by entering an apprenticeship program. These programs are offered through the trade union, the prospective employer, or the state department of education. Educational and organizing programs for women are slowly gaining ground. The Coalition of Labor Union Women (CLUW) is an interunion organization founded in 1973 to provide a forum for discussing common concerns and seeking solutions to these problems.

Paraprofessional work is another nontraditional area that has been opening up to midlife women. The rising cost of professional services and in some fields a demand for these services that exceeds the supply have given impetus to the occupation of paraprofessional, or "para." So far, paraprofessionals, acting as a bridge between busy professionals and the public, have been finding their best opportunities in the legal profession. As the cost of hiring a lawyer has risen beyond the reach of the average person's income, the paraprofessional provides an important service by taking over tasks that would otherwise have to be performed by the lawyer, thus making it possible for the fees to be substantially lower. Paralegals draft legal documents, comfort clients, sort and catalog data, schedule meetings, and gather information. They cannot appear in court or give legal advice.

The age factor that is one of the determining criteria in the hiring of law clerks is less important for paras. A paralegal might resemble any of these:

A 55-year-old woman, recently widowed, whose work experience consisted of part-time jobs as a legal secretary. She completed the paralegal program while working at one of these jobs and then was hired immediately by the same firm as a full-time paralegal.

A 49-year-old woman, married, with an ailing husband. She had little work experience, mostly with volunteer organizations. "I was always interested in law. If I were 10 years younger, I would go to law school. For me now, the paralegal program is a realistic alternative." During the course, one of her instructors who was a partner in a law firm was impressed by her outstanding work and hired her when she completed the program.

A 50-year-old woman who had been doing general office work since her divorce 10 years ago. She took a bank loan to put herself through the paralegal program and now has a well-paying job with a respected firm in the Los Angeles area.

Other fields that are beginning to make use of paraprofessionals are veterinary medicine, social work, and the health sciences. As professional services expand and become increasingly specialized, paras will be much in demand, and competence on the job will make the age factor increasingly irrelevant.

PART-TIME WORK

A full-time job is not always the most desirable option for women who want to work. Part-time employment may better suit someone who still has domestic responsibilities, is caring for aging parents, or simply does not want to invest as much of her time and energy as a full-time job requires. Another advantage to part-time work is that in times of an economic slowdown, it is more readily available.

Part-time jobs come in all sizes and shapes and offer all degrees of personal satisfaction. They are more likely to be found among traditional occupations; most are low-paying; and the chances for advancement are virtually nil. But they offer a means of picking up some extra money, sharpening unused skills, and serving as a transition between home and workplace. Here are a few examples of part-time jobs that offer flexible work schedules:

* Temporary Work. Part-time office work obtained through agencies specializing in temporary office help.

* Job Pairing. Two women divide one full-time job with each responsible for half of the job.

* Split-Level Job. A position is divided into two levels of training or ability; the employer hires two part-time employees with different skill levels to provide full-time coverage and pays them in accordance with their skills.

* Flex-time Job. The job may be done partly at the office and partly at home. The computer is making this type of arrangement more feasible for employers and employees. It is ideal for women who want to work at a full-time job but are still needed at home.

JOB-SEEKING STRATEGIES

When, after a careful analysis of your needs, skills, and options, you have arrived at a decision about the kind of job that is best for you, you are ready to develop a job-seeking plan. The résumé, your self-portrait in words, is the key strategy in your job search. A well-written résumé should state your skills and accomplishments clearly and succinctly and should be carefully aimed at the specific requirements of the job you are applying for. Include your educational background: academic and other degrees as well as credits toward a degree and your major; all your work experience, paid or unpaid; honors, awards, memberships, any relevant hobbies or interests. To counter any possible age bias, present yourself as healthy and dynamic and with no intention of taking early retirement. Your résumé should sell you to the prospective employer without falsifying or exaggerating your qualifications.

For women who are in transition between traditional and contemporary values, self-promotion can be a major stumbling block in their job search. A woman in her early 50s who grew up in a small town in Ohio told me that in her family the girls were taught to be modest and never to utter a word that could be construed as self-praise. "It was OK for my brothers to brag about their batting averages and their sexual conquests, but for my sisters and me, it was another story. Putting yourself forward, we were told, is unfeminine."

Since this woman is employed in a management position and exudes self-confidence, I asked her how she had overcome the restraints that had been imposed upon her. "I went into therapy for a while, and that helped. But what really did it for me was joining a women's support group. It made me realize how many women had this problem, and I'm talking about women who you'd swear had it all — looks, marriage, career. We gave each other the strength we needed to go after what we wanted. We also exchanged information about job leads and edited each other's résumés."

Your résumé should be professionally typed or laser printed. If you are mailing it, enclose a brief cover letter, addressed to the appropriate person, in which you state that you will call in a few days. When you make your follow-up call, ask for an appointment. Your next step is to research the company and the job as part of your preparation for the interview.

THE POWER OF THE IMAGE

Preparing for a job interview is an exercise in self-confrontation, particularly for middle-aged women who are returning to the workplace after several years of full-time homemaking. A 54-year-old woman who complained about being repeatedly turned down for jobs which, as she bemoaned, "were made to order for me," described herself to a career counselor as "20 pounds overweight, wear a 15-year-old coat, and cut my own hair." This self-portrait is enough to explain why she was still looking for a job after 24 interviews.

We live in an age of images. In the workplace and especially in the executive suite, the idealized images that are projected by movies and television serve as standards for corporate hiring practices. "Few executives realize how critically important their physical appearance may be to an employer," writes Erving Goffman in *The Presentation of Self in Everyday Life*. "Placement expert Ann Hoff observes that employers now seem to be looking for an ideal 'Hollywood type.' One company rejected a candidate because he had 'teeth that were too square' and others have been disqualified because their ears stuck out . . ."

Although skills and training are the essential prerequisites in today's job market, appearance can be a decisive factor when the choice is between several equally qualified candidates. Midlife women who have been full-time homemakers have been occupied with the needs of others—husbands, children, aging parents; they often do not realize that they have neglected themselves and have lost sight of how they appear to others outside of their circle of family and friends. Women who have been in this situation and who eventually were hired for jobs at the management level maintain that the best investment they ever made was in a program of self-rejuvenation, which included diet and exercise, hair coloring and styling, and an updated wardrobe.

One woman who, after several turndowns, listened to herself on tape, could hardly believe what she heard: "I was listening to the mumbling voice of an old woman. It was a bit of a shock." She went to a speech therapist, who helped her develop a youthful, vibrant tone and crisp enunciation. It took several months and it was hard work, but she said, "It was worth it. It gave me confidence, made me feel like a new woman." She is now employed as assistant director of a management-training program.

QUESTIONS AND ANSWERS

The interview is your opportunity to present yourself in a positive way, emphasizing your abilities, training, experience, and how they apply specifically to the job. Be prepared for challenging questions, such as:

Why do you think you are right for this job? If you have done your homework and know something about the company and the kind of person they are looking for, this type of question should not present any difficulty. Answer in a concise and straightforward manner and emphasize how your training, skills, and experience will be helpful to the company.

How will you feel about working with people in their 20s and 30s? Your response to this one should focus on your energy and commitment to the goals of the job. Here is where you can make a strong case for the advantages of maturity and experience.

What kind of salary are you expecting? It is advisable not to state an exact figure at this stage. You can say that you want to learn more about the job and that the salary is negotiable.

If you are turned down, don't take it personally. Even in times of economic prosperity, there is tough competition for desirable jobs. As a woman in midlife, you may feel that you have an especially difficult hurdle to overcome, but on the credit side of the ledger are the special resources — self-help groups, employment centers, job clubs, and networks — that have been springing up around the country to help mature job seekers.

The self-help club known as Forty Plus is located in 17 cities, including New York, Philadelphia, and Denver. Operation ABLE (Ability Based on Long Experience) is a network of community-based employment centers that provide services, most of which are free, to midlifers who are seeking employment. Write to Operation ABLE, 36 South Wabash Avenue, Chicago, IL 60603. AARP Works is a pilot employment-planning program consisting of job-search workshops. The American Association of Retired Persons offered AARP Works in 16 cities in 1988 and is planning to expand it throughout the country in the 1990s. For further information, write to Work

Force Education, AARP Worker Equity Department, 1909 K Street, NW, Washington, DC 20049. Local resources include your state department of employment, state department of human resources, career counseling centers, women's resource centers, community colleges, adult education programs.

Whether you are considering a traditional or a nontraditional career, careful planning and preparation should lead you to the job of your choice. You'll find the opportunities if you know where to look for them and how to make the most of them.

&

CHAPTER SEVEN

The Midlife
Career Crisis

&

SEVEN

A prerequisite for a successful life is a capacity for change, for new learning. If you have that capacity, you can learn a new job.
Catherine Bateson, <u>Working Woman</u>, May 1990

A Boston advertising copywriter decides to quit her high-salaried position and moves to a small town in Vermont, where she writes articles for the local paper and works on a novel that she has been planning for several years.

A facilities engineer in Los Angeles loses her job and becomes a designer of mechanical toys.

A court reporter based in a midwestern city moves to the Southwest, where she earns a teaching degree and is hired to teach English as a second language (ESL) by the community college.

A public-health official in Cincinnati takes early retirement and works out of her home as a consultant, advising executives on stress management.

A public-relations executive for an oil company in Philadelphia leaves her job to become ordained as the first female bishop of the Episcopal church.

An elementary school teacher goes into therapy to seek help for depression and discovers that her true vocation is the practice of psychotherapy.

A Hollywood actress who has won an Oscar and two Emmys switches from acting to directing.

What do these women, who live in very different worlds and come from very different backgrounds, have in common? They are all in their middle years, and they have all made a major midlife career change. Switching careers in midstream was almost unheard-of when these women were in their 20s. The traditional approach to career preparation was based on the assumption that this was a decision for your life's work. A woman who overcame the odds and achieved success in her chosen career would not have considered trading in her hard-won position for another type of occupation, especially when she was in her 40s or 50s. She would have felt that there was not enough time left for a major life change.

But today, our lifelines have been stretched, making possible many acts, roles, and scene changes. Careers, like marriages, are no longer regarded as immutable. We change our occupations as we change our marital status and often for similar reasons: Because *we* have changed and need to move in a new direction, or because we want to find meaning and purpose to fill an empty space in our lives. The gnawing dissatisfaction that prompts a woman in her middle years to ask "What am I doing in this marriage?" may also cause her to wonder "What am I doing in this job?"

For most women, the midlife career crisis is actually a crisis of identity, a moment of truth, of self-confrontation. Who am I? What do I want out of life? These questions can no longer be avoided. The rationalizations that buoyed up our choices in the past no longer work. Our children are or will soon be on their own. Our financial pressures are or could be reduced. We have found ways to cope with family and personal problems.

We have earned the right to freedom without guilt. And we appreciate more than ever the preciousness of time, the importance of using it to our best advantage.

And yet the midlife career switch is an act of brinkmanship. It requires willpower and the capacity for risk-taking. It requires a sense of adventure and the courage to challenge the generally accepted view of middle age as a time for settling down, a time for stability and continuity, especially for women.

Women have not been encouraged to initiate change, states Catherine Bateson, anthropologist and college administrator. In an interview in the magazine *Working Woman*, she observes that women have a hard time making changes in their lives. The innovators, the pioneers, have been men. "Women often feel a responsibility to keep things on an even keel. They do not act for change. Rather, they let change happen to them. They don't seem to realize that their first job is probably temporary, that they're going to end up going on to something else — perhaps something different. The effect of this kind of career focus is that they may prepare themselves too narrowly for the shifts they will encounter in the course of their lives."

REASONS FOR A CAREER CHANGE

But resistance to change is part of the psychological baggage that midlife women are shedding as they establish themselves in their careers. In the executive ranks, women today are more mobile than men. The median job tenure for a woman manager is five years, in contrast to a man's seven, according to the Bureau of Labor Statistics. And the popular assumption that women leave their jobs to return to domesticity has no basis in fact. A survey by Wick and Company, a consulting firm, found that, like men, most women move on to advance their careers. Only 7 percent of the women surveyed left their jobs to return to homemaking. Many quit to set up their own firms. In 1987, women owned more than twice as many companies as they did 10 years earlier.

In these volatile times, being able to adapt to change is the first law of economic survival. But for midlife women who have had to break through barriers to establish themselves in their careers, change doesn't come easily. Among the women I interviewed, there were those who would like to change careers but were held back by their fear of the unknown. Why, they wanted to know, would a woman in her middle years walk away from a career in which she has invested many years of training and hard work? Isn't it risky at this age to take that kind of leap?

When I questioned women who had made a midlife career change about their reasons, they cited burnout almost as often as career advancement. They described the symptoms accompanying burnout as restlessness; loss of interest in the job; no pride or gratification in what you accomplish; fatigue and a constant feeling of boredom while at work; frustration; no interest in the job outside of the paycheck; increased tension in relations with family and coworkers; stress-related ailments. Burnout may simply signify that the job itself is lacking in substance and offers little or no challenge.

This need for a new challenge is frequently the impetus behind a midlife career change. Actress Lee Grant, who in her late 50s has been making the transition from acting to directing, finds stimulation in overcoming tough obstacles. In Hollywood, the barriers against women directors have been virtually insurmountable, but Grant considers that the rise and fall on the way to her goal is "a normal part of my life, one that I really like because obstacles are very challenging to me."

She also credits other women directors who have paved the way. "There really have been some charming and important and successful movies done in the last five years by women," she says, citing such directors as Gillian Armstrong, Penny

Marshall, Randa Haines, and Joan Silver. "They really did it. They made it possible for me."

Giving Birth to Yourself

For some women, a midlife career change is a response to unmet inner needs. A 52-year-old psychotherapist made the decision to switch careers while she was in therapy. She was employed as a substitute elementary school teacher and suffered from recurring attacks of depression. "It was a difficult time in my life. The death of my father hit me hard. I felt more conscious of time passing; my life was going by and what was I doing with it? I've always enjoyed children, but I knew teaching wasn't right for me. And yet, I had no idea what I really wanted to do. It was as if part of me was locked away and I couldn't get to it. And then one day my therapist gave me the key. She told me, 'You're trying to give birth to something. Why don't you give birth to yourself?'

"I suddenly realized what I wanted to do. I wanted to be a therapist. I enrolled in a two-year course of study, then went into private practice with supervision. I'm licensed now and practicing on my own. I can't imagine anything more satisfying than this work. To be able to help people cope with their problems—what could be more rewarding? And in this field, age is an advantage. The older you are, the better you are, because you're working from a broader base of knowledge and experience."

A Healthy Push

In an uncertain job market, a change of occupation in midlife is often the result of corporate downsizing, a euphemism for wholesale firing which invariably accompanies a downturn in the economy. Older employees are usually the first to go. (Some companies offer incentives, such as an upgraded retirement plan, to encourage longtime employees to leave.) But becoming unemployed after many years in the same job can have a positive effect; it can provide a healthy push to move in a new career direction.

The 55-year-old facilities engineer referred to at the beginning of this chapter lost her job during a drastic staff reduction. After months of fruitless job searching, she decided that it was time to change careers. She is now designing mechanical toys for a large toy manufacturer. "I was ready for a change, but I wouldn't have had the guts to leave," she told me. "Getting fired was the best thing that ever happened to me."

A Job Is Not a Life

A midlife career switch may be motivated by life changes or a shift in personal priorities: a husband's job transfer to another geographic area; the desire for a less time-consuming job to allow for more social and cultural activities; an opportunity to live closer to children and grandchildren; or, as it was for a 49-year-old court reporter, a form of compensation for her childlessness. As the older of two sisters, she was expected to be the first to marry and provide her parents with grandchildren. "But it didn't work out that way," she told me. "I had my share of affairs, but I was in love, really in love, only once. We lived together for three years, best years of my life, but then he decided to go back to his wife—said he missed his kids. So that was that.

"I figured in many ways I was lucky. I had good friends, a lot of interests, and I liked my job as a court reporter. It was demanding, but it paid well, and it was never dull. So why did I decide to leave it and start a new career?

"It was when I turned 45 and went into what my gynecologist said was early menopause. The biological message was coming through loud and clear; it was telling me I'd never have a child. I hadn't thought of myself as especially maternal, but now all I could think about was how much I wanted to have a child. Seeing children playing on the street or with their mothers in the supermarket was enough to make the tears come.

"I began rethinking my life, toyed with the idea of adoption, but it didn't sit right with me. Maybe I'm too family-oriented to take on a child that wasn't of my flesh and blood. Then my sister's husband walked out on her, and when she called me in hysterics, I knew what I had to do. I took a leave of absence from my job and flew to Houston to try to comfort her.

"While I was staying with her, I took over with the kids, my eight-year-old nephew and five-year-old niece. It gave Ellen the space she needed to pull herself together. And it brought back the closeness we used to have. I got so attached to the kids, I decided to move to Houston so I could be near them.

"I could have gone back to court reporting, but I was ready for something that wasn't so time and energy consuming. A job is not a life. I'd always known that, but I decided it was time to do something about it. With the large immigrant population in the area, there was a need for teachers of English as a second language. English was always my best subject in school, so I had no trouble getting the credential. And now I'm teaching in the community college.

"Funny how Ellen and I both changed our lives in midstream. And we feel stronger and more in control than ever before. Since Ellen had to take a full-time job and I have flexible hours, I can help out with the kids. Our parents are dead now, and I'm sorry I didn't have the marriage or the children they hoped for. I'll never be a mother, but I'm an aunt. That's almost as good."

Seeing the Light

Taking off in a new career direction in midlife can actually signify a turning back to recapture former aspirations. When Barbara Harris, a 58-year-old divorced black woman and civil-rights activist, was ordained as the first female bishop of the

Episcopal church, she was breaking new ground as well as asserting her commitment to the priorities of her early years. In Barbara's case, she could not have followed a straight path to her present position because the church did not ordain women as priests until 1974.

In 1980, after 22 years as a public relations executive in her native Philadelphia, she quit to become a priest. "She worked for a living, but she lived for the church," said the man she calls her mentor, the Reverend Paul Washington. Now a typical day in her life includes presiding over services, attending church receptions, and visiting a shelter for homeless pregnant women. She is also executive director of the Episcopal Church Publishing Company, an umbrella group that publishes the *Witness*, a church journal. Her schedule is demanding and often exhausting, and her liberal political views have made her a figure of controversy, but there is no doubt that this is a woman who has found her personal truth and is living up to the best in herself by constantly reaching beyond where she is at the moment.

Harris admits that she had been dubious about women becoming priests, but over time, as she herself evolved and developed self-confidence, her thinking changed. Now when she is asked what made her choose in her late 40s a vocation which requires such preparation and dedication, she responds simply, "I saw the light."

For many women, achieving success in a career has been a broadening and deepening experience. For others, it has had the opposite effect, confining them within a narrow structure that puts a clamp on their talents and energies. The competitive arena of the corporate world tends to discourage any form of creative expression that does not directly advance the company's goals. "Seeing the light" then becomes a struggle to break out of these restricting boundaries and rediscover ourselves.

CAN I AFFORD TO MAKE THE CHANGE?

Before deciding to change careers, women in their middle years should make a careful self-assessment of their needs, their skills, and their financial situation. Upfront questions that should be addressed are:

How much salary do I really need?

What kind of work satisfaction am I seeking?

Would I be willing to move to another part of the country?

When a 52-year-old advertising copywriter wrestled with these questions, the answers she came up with assured her that she could safely make the change she had been thinking about for several years. On the surface, she appeared to be in an enviable position. The company she worked for was one of New England's fastest-growing advertising agencies. Her salary provided her with a comfortable house, domestic help, and college educations for her children. She had more than 20 years of experience in advertising and was valued by her employers. Why would she want to give up a career in which she had invested so many years and that offered so many advantages?

Behind the having-it-all facade was the story of a woman who had been living, as she put it, "someone else's life." She had always wanted to be a writer and had made several starts at writing a novel, but marriage, children, and her husband's early death meant that she had to devote herself full-time to the support of the family. She found a job in advertising, and, thanks to her writing skill, she was rapidly promoted to a top position in copywriting. Now, with only one of her children in college, she saw a chance to reduce her expenses and realize her lifelong dream. She was poised at a now-or-never crossroads, and she knew that if she didn't take that other road at this moment in her life, she never would.

It meant making drastic changes, but she had long ago lost whatever interest her job had held for her and, having grown up in a small rural community, she had never fully adapted to the fast pace and impersonality of urban life. Now happily settled in a small farming town in Vermont, she writes articles for the local paper and has nearly finished the first draft of her novel. Reaching back into her past gave her the impetus to redefine herself for the future she had always wanted.

REDEFINING YOURSELF

In the process of changing careers, we often discover aspects of ourselves that we had not suspected. When I was working in public relations, I felt that I owed my job solely to my writing skills. I detached myself from all other aspects of the field, such as marketing and client relations, convinced that I had nothing to offer in these areas. Years later, when I made my midlife career switch to adult education, I discovered aptitudes that had been lying dormant within me: the ability to counsel students, work with professors and university administrators, design educational programs, manage complex budgets.

It's not easy for people to think of their skills and talents beyond the boundaries of their job, claims Charles Handy, a visiting professor at the London Business School and a writer on organizational change. "We all have a lot of neglected talents. It's a matter of redefining yourself. You need help because you've only seen yourself in one light." He suggests that, when you are thinking about a job change, you can free up your thinking about your capabilities by asking several people you know to tell you what they think you do best. Seeing yourself through the eyes of others can reveal aptitudes you were not aware of.

Handy warns that the result of this type of survey may surprise you. He cites the case of a 44-year-old advertising executive who had just lost his job. The man followed Handy's instructions and found the results of his informal questionnaire "sort of embarrassing." Out of the 20 answers, not one was advertising. Instead, he was told that he was creative, good at organizing teams, presenting ideas, leading people, selecting wines, and recalling historical details. He has set up his own business, conducting tours of historical sites throughout Europe. "A nice example of what you can do with some original thinking," comments Handy.

Viewing your skills in a new and expanded way can be difficult for many women who, by the time they reach midlife, have performed so many different tasks at home and at work that they are unsure about where their strengths lie and what their preferences are. A self-assessment process can be helpful in shaping a new career focus.

A good way to start the process, according to the Greenwich Group, an outplacement company, is by writing an autobiography, breaking it up into chapters: early childhood, grade school, high school, college, first job, second job, and so on. This becomes a basis for analyzing where, along the way, you were at your best and were truly enjoying what you were doing. Out of this analysis, you can begin to formulate a plan of action based on those skills and aspirations that best fit the growth areas in the economy.

PROSPECTS FOR THE FUTURE

Economist and employment specialists see five trends that are significant for women considering a midlife career change: a major restructuring of the workplace with less emphasis on hierarchical levels and closer working relationships between employees and management, and shifts toward self-employment, working at home, smaller companies, and employment of older workers. Most of the job growth today comes from small companies because, according to James Challenger, president of a Chicago outplacement company, "What a smaller organization wants is someone who can wear three or four hats. People over 50 are more likely to have the necessary experience."

Looking ahead, the most promising fields appear to be those that require some specialized training or experience or a combination of the two. Accounting is a growth area, with opportunities in both public and private sectors. Prerequisites are a bachelor's degree with a major or minor in accounting; a CPA degree is not necessary but is considered an asset. In the computer industry, jobs in software and hardware development are expected to double. Formal training is not required, but it is important to have some background and experience in mathematics and computer sciences.

Food management is growing in large urban areas, with hotels, hospitals, and major restaurant chains always on the lookout for experienced chefs and food managers. Training generally takes two years or more, and on-the-job experience is highly valued. Other good prospects in which experience counts for more than training or degrees are personnel work, sales, export-import, and public relations.

Home Is Where the Work Is

Women who still have domestic responsibilities or who are tired of long commutes on traffic-choked highways or who simply want more control over their time and energy are taking advantage of emerging opportunities to work at home. Thanks to the computer, the fax machine, and other electronic devices, working at home is becoming a realistic option in a growing number of commercial enterprises. In an information age, in which many jobs involve the transfer and manipulation of information, working at home makes good economic sense. Employers can recruit from a larger pool of talent, make greater use of part-time employees, and benefit from reduced demands for office space and parking facilities.

Today more than 26 million Americans, 23 percent of the total work force, are working at home. The two main groups are entrepreneurs who run businesses from home and employees who work at home under an arrangement with their companies.

Women now account for 70 percent of all home-based proprietorships. They are managing commodities funds, publishing newsletters, designing sportswear, doing research, advising and consulting in many areas. Though working mothers have given the greatest impetus to the trend, women in their post-motherhood years are also finding advantages in working at home. It provides more flexibility, frees them from the stresses of commuting and the confinement of an office, and allows them to work at their own pace and at a number of projects at a time, even for more than one employer.

Becoming a franchisee is an attractive option for women who are considering a midlife career switch since it lets them start out with an already established business. "Franchise companies are beating a path to their door," says John Reynolds of the International Franchise Association, "because these women offer past business experience, stability, and motivation." Franchisees who set up their own businesses receive company training and benefit from national advertising, name recognition, and bulk rates for their supplies.

The Isolation Factor

Despite its advantages, combining home and work is not always a utopian solution to women's career problems. Working mothers must cope with the tensions of tending children while attempting to concentrate on the job at hand. Midlife women whose children are gone and whose home is now quiet and peaceful — on the face of it an ideal situation — are confronted by the isolation factor. While the working mother can alleviate her problem with the help of day care and baby-sitters, resources for dealing with isolation are not so readily available.

For many women, especially those who have been full-time homemakers, a job means more than a paycheck. It gives them an opportunity to escape from the enclosed world of the domestic realm to an interactive environment. People work for many reasons aside from money. Some are social, some are psychological. There is more to the workplace, whether it is an office or a factory or a movie set, than the actual work that is performed there. It is also a place where people meet, exchange ideas and information, and learn how to function in a social setting, where friendships are formed and love affairs blossom. "People need to affiliate with others," affirms Dr. Mary Ann Van Glinow, who teaches a course on women in management at the University of Southern California, "and that's a real, vital function of organizations that they don't always think through."

For middle-aged women who are just beginning to move up in the corporate hierarchy, working at home has another downside. "Part of the way people get promoted in an organization is visibility," Von Glinow emphasizes, "and when you are off-site, you are not visible. So you take yourself out of the game."

If, after considering the trade-offs, working at home still looks like the best of all possible arrangements, you can take some steps to head off a feeling of isolation. Before you make the move from workplace to home, ask yourself: Will I miss my contacts with colleagues? Will I feel lonely, cut off from office gossip and politics, from meetings and planning sessions? Will I feel extraneous to the day-to-day life of the organization? Will my job performance suffer because of the lack of stimulation from colleagues?

If your answers are a clear and resounding yes, you can make some plans to stay involved with the people and activities that are important to you and relevant to your work. Women who are enjoying the benefits of working at home while maintaining their personal linkages with the job offer these suggestions:

* Set up a regular schedule of lunch dates with the people who have been your most compatible colleagues.

* Request that you be included in meetings even if they have only a marginal relevance to your work.

* Form a committee of other at-home workers and arrange to meet with appropriate staff in order to exchange ideas and information.

* From time to time, invite people from the organization — or client organizations if you are working for more than one company — to your home for informal social occasions.

* Working at home may not be a panacea for every woman who is going through a midlife career crisis, but for those who want the privacy and independence of home along with the stimulation and social interaction of the workplace, the new working-at-home trend offers an opportunity to combine the best of both worlds.

Changing careers in midstream requires careful planning and forethought. It is not the kind of decision that should be made on impulse. Given time, a feeling of restlessness or dissatisfaction with your job may turn out to be a transitory mood or a symptom of something that is amiss in another area of your life, rather than in your career. But whichever path you decide to follow at this critical juncture, being able to adapt to change will serve you well in meeting the challenges of these unpredictable times.

CHAPTER EIGHT

૨૪

Moneywise
Women

૨૪

EIGHT

Many aspects of women's lives at midlife are problematic. Among the most notable features is an economic vulnerability that derives directly from a combination of work and family history.

Judy Long and Karen L. Porter,
"Multiple Roles of Midlife Women"

When I was growing up, the two subjects that were taboo for the women in my family were sex and money. From the storehouse of memory, I can recall a scene that was a backdrop to my early years: my mother, my grandmother, and my aunts gathered around the kitchen table sipping tea and talking animatedly about food, religion, the problems with husbands and children, current neighborhood scandals, and the peccadilloes of family members. Sometimes these discussions dissolved into squeals of laughter at a funny story about a friend or relative. But in neither the serious nor the lighter side of these women-only forums was there ever a passing mention of bodily functions or financial matters. These topics had no place in the conversation of decent, feminine women, and they were relegated to the male side of the family.

As I look back, I realize that it was the women in the family who managed the day-to-day budgets, who haggled with neighborhood merchants, and who set aside funds for the children's education and occasional holidays at the seashore. But it was assumed that the men were in charge of the family finances, since women were too soft and sensitive to deal with something as crass as money.

The more things change, the more they remain the same, as the French saying goes. And for some things, change is so slow, it is almost imperceptible. In these post-sexual-revolution years, there are women over 50 who can talk more freely about sex than about money. Here is a 55-year-old librarian commenting on her close-knit circle of women friends: "I can assure you, we know more about each other's sex lives than about our personal and family finances."

Women who have been sheltered from hard economic facts by their fathers and later their husbands often find themselves, after divorce or widowhood, struggling to comprehend such mysteries as tax shelters, annuities, mutual funds, IRAs, stocks, bonds, mortgages, 401-K plans. In *Financial Self-Confidence for the Suddenly Single*, Alan B. Ungar, C.F.P. (certified financial planner), reports that when women are forced to take over the management of their finances, their fears come through loud and clear:

- "I don't understand money."
- "I'm scared!"
- "He made all the financial decisions."
- "I hate thinking about money!"
- "I want somebody else to do it."

Elizabeth Slocum, a 51-year-old marriage and family counselor, reports that her women clients are more often troubled by unsatisfactory relationships with money than with men. She says that midlife women, especially, have been taught that it is unfeminine to talk about money. Some are virtually moneyphobic. Acknowledging the ambivalence of the midlife woman who is juggling two sets of money values, she advises her clients to overcome their fiscal inhibitions by discussing economic issues with friends, boning up on personal finance, and finding a financial mentor. Slocum admits it took her a long time to be able to say to her friends, "'I want to make $100,000 a year.' It sounds greedy and not very nice." She advises her clients to overcome their fiscal inhibitions by discussing economic issues with friends, boning up on personal finance, and finding a financial mentor.

CHANGING YOUR MONEY HABITS

Women who are new to personal money management may have to change their money habits, not an easy thing to do since the way we manage money is embedded deep in our culture. The American attitude toward money is that it can not only buy happiness but can order it custom-made in any size, shape, or quantity desired. And for women, Descartes' principle, "I think, therefore I am," has been revised to, "I shop, therefore I am." Women often judge each other, especially on early acquaintance, by outward appearance — by the trimness of the figure, the stylishness of the hair, the fit and fashion of the clothes.

I Shop, Therefore I Am

Shopping for clothes and cosmetics can serve as an affirmation of a woman's sexuality, especially when she is going through menopause. "The way women sexualize their spending," writes Thomas Wiseman in his book *The Money Motive*, "is in the sudden irrational spending spree. In its classic form this is usually the outcome of a simmering emotional tension, which explodes in a bout of heedless extravagance, in which things are bought that are later found to be useless or unneeded."

From an early age, we are encouraged to invest more in our external appearance than in our inner development, but as we leave youth behind us, the message is reinforced with subtle and not-so-subtle threats and warnings. A glance at the ads in the media reflect the cosmetics and fashion trades' general perception of women as susceptible to any product, regardless of price, that promises to counteract signs of age. "Smooths away wrinkles," the copy proclaims, "covers the gray," "makes you look years younger." And alongside these messages are those from plastic surgeons, offering to remove eye pouches, repair sagging cheeks, buoy up drooping breasts, and remodel virtually any part of the face or body that suggests it has been touched by the passing of time.

Women in their middle years are especially susceptible to the narcissism that the cosmetic and fashion industries encourage. Imbued with age-consciousness, they know they can no longer rely on nature for their most valued attribute — youthful attractiveness. During these middle years, when there are so many losses and crises to contend with, shopping often becomes a form of therapy. "When I'm depressed," one woman told me, "I buy a new outfit." Adding a new dress, a new hat, an expensive piece of jewelry to her already extensive wardrobe is a familiar coping strategy for the woman who can afford to indulge her moods with lavish expenditures.

But after all, isn't she simply responding to messages that have been beamed at her since childhood? In a money-driven society in which materialism supersedes spiritual values, hasn't she been assured that fulfillment and true happiness can be hers if she is a skillful consumer? I have heard of a nursing home that includes a trip to a nearby shopping mall in its regular schedule of weekly activities; although the women do not need the merchandise and have very little money to spend, they feel younger and more alive, as though they are part of life's mainstream when they are mingling with throngs of shoppers.

But, you might ask, what if it makes me feel better to look my best, to dress well, and have an attractive home? Why shouldn't I spend money to make myself feel good? What's the problem? The problem is that when spending becomes an addiction, a way of dealing with pain and disappointment and self-dissatisfaction, it can erode the strength and the resources you need to confront yourself honestly, which you must do before you can resolve your difficulties. Also, it is unwise for middle-aged women to become dependent on a level of spending which they may not be able to maintain during this time of critical life changes.

"Women spend five times as much money on clothes as men do," notes Emily Card, a lawyer, financial consultant, and the author of the *Ms. Money Book*. "There is a lot of pressure on women to dress well. I don't think we have to blame women for that, but we can make do with less clothes. I think women, especially middle-class women, have fallen into a trap. They are trying to prove they have more than they do."

From Spending to Saving

Card suggests that women set realistic savings goals, saving 5 percent to 10 percent of their yearly salary. In her book, she offers these spend-and-save recommendations:

* If your clothing expenses exceed 5 percent of your income, shift the remainder to savings.

* No more than 3 percent to 4 percent of your total income should go to vacations. If you haven't purchased a home, redirect vacation funds to a home down-payment fund.

* If dining out has put your food bill at 10 percent of your gross income or above, cut back.

❖ Don't buy a new car if you haven't bought a home.

❖ Recheck your insurance policy. You can save 1 percent to 2 percent of your income by eliminating unnecessary insurance.

Financial advisers offer these additional suggestions:

❖ Develop your goals for saving—retirement, travel, college costs for children, the needs of aging parents. Set up a schedule for meeting those goals.

❖ Make savings automatic. You can do this by joining a credit union and having a specified amount of money deposited directly from your paycheck into your savings account. Or you can arrange for a mutual fund to withdraw an agreed-upon amount from your checking or savings account.

❖ Pay off your credit-card debt. Few if any investments will pay dividends approaching the high rate of interest charged by most credit-card companies.

❖ Figure out what percentage of your earnings you have been saving this year and increase it in the coming year by as much as you can without cutting into your basic needs.

Changing your habits from spending to saving may force you to face up to questions that you have been evading, such as: What are my real needs? Why do I go on shopping binges? What nonessentials can I trim from my shopping list? What am I trying to buy my way out of—or into? If you feel you can't resist the occasional impulse to splurge on luxuries, financial consultant Lawrence A. Krause suggests that you play a game with yourself: Pretend that your rent or mortgage or car payment has been increased; once you've made these actual payments, put the "increase" into your savings account, or as a further safety measure, into a less readily accessible place, such as a U.S. savings bond that matures in five or more years.

Krause offers this guide for building a nest egg: Approximately 50 percent of your assets should be readily accessible in money-market accounts, savings accounts, or stocks that have immediate cash value. Another 25 percent should be in semiliquid investments, such as deferred annuities, with the remaining 25 percent in "assets you can afford to tie up," such as real estate.

Money and Power

Financial security in today's economy is an illusion, a woman who is an investment counselor told me recently. She might have added, "especially for midlife women." Imbued with the traditional view that a concern with money is unfeminine, they do not connect money with the personal power that gives them the freedom to make their own choices and act on them. "Women don't think about making a lot of money and having power like men do," says Esther Worthington, vice-president of International Credit Professionals in St. Louis. "That's why women entrepreneurs are few and far between."

But women who make the connection between money and personal power and want to start their own small businesses are faced with the problem of obtaining the necessary credit. Although women are the backbone of small businesses, Emily Card, who helped draft the U.S. Equal Credit Opportunity Act of 1974, refers to Small Business Administration studies which show that women still don't get as large a line of credit or as favorable terms as men get.

Access to credit is basic to business in today's financial climate, yet this is an area of money management in which many midlife women lack the sophistication of younger generations of women. "Many older married women still haven't established their own credit identity," says Gerri Detweiler of the Bankcard Holders of America, a consumer education group based in Herndon, Virginia. "The card may have her own name on it, but she may not be legally liable because it is not a joint account that she had to sign for. In that case, she is an authorized user but does not have credit in her name." A divorce or the death of her husband can confront her with many difficulties.

MONEY IN MARRIAGE

In the not-so-distant past, a financially stable marriage was regarded as a woman's lifetime protection from money problems, but that assumption is no longer valid. A roller-coaster economy and the high divorce rate have eroded any expectations of financial security in marriage that women may have carried over from their traditional upbringing. The breakup of a marriage can spell financial disaster for the woman. The average income of a woman after divorce or separation falls about 37 percent within four months of the breakup. A recent Census Bureau study reported that marital dissolution is followed by a doubling in welfare dependency and by an increase in women holding full-time jobs from 33 percent before the separation to 41 percent afterward.

Women who have maintained their careers throughout their marriage are less affected financially by the breakup of their marriage, although the loss of a second income may necessitate some budgetary cutbacks. It is the full-time homemakers who usually find themselves in a precarious financial position after divorce. Too often, women who have lived within a sheltered domestic environment have been content to remain ignorant about the family finances, and their husbands have made no effort to enlighten them. "My husband refused to discuss money with me," is a typical comment from women who were in traditional marriages in which the husband was the sole earner.

"I had a good marriage," a 54-year-old waitress told me during an interview. "My husband was a welder, and he earned good money. We brought up three children. We owned our house free and clear, or so I thought. I stayed home, took care of the house and kids. I left all the money business to him. I knew he liked to gamble, but I figured, well, better that than drink or other women. So what if he went to the races once in a while or played cards with the boys? He worked hard, he had a right to enjoy himself in his own way.

"Then he had a heart attack at work, and two weeks later he was dead. And I found out that he had taken out a mortgage on the house to support his gambling. And there were a lot of other debts that started coming due, not all from gambling. There was also a woman, and I never had a suspicion. My kids helped me as best they could, but they're married and have their own families and their own problems. I didn't want to depend on them. I'd never worked for pay, didn't know how to do much, so I've got this job, saving every penny I can, trying to hang on to my house. That's all I want. That's my security, my house, where I lived for 30 years and raised my kids."

Getting to Know Your Finances

If your husband has been keeping a tight hold on the family purse strings, you might suggest that, at this point in your lives, it is important for both of you to do some estate planning. Set up a meeting with your attorney and insist on having every-thing explained to you. An additional safeguard would be a written agreement, spelling out the financial arrangements in the event of divorce. This type of agreement, known as a pre-nuptial contract, is a common feature in second marriages in which allocations are made for the merging of property and other assets.

Experts advise women in their middle years, whatever their marital situation, to get acquainted with their finances. Women who suddenly find themselves on their own can turn to a fi-nancial consultant for help, but they will be better served by a professional if they have a thorough knowledge of their financial affairs. Micheline Lamotta, a CPA who is controller of a video distribution company, recommends the following course of action:

Make a list of income sources and obligations, such as rent or mortgage, utilities, medical expenses, debts, insurance, transportation, food, recreation, and entertainment.

Determine whether your income covers your obligations. Make a thorough search for any statements that might be filed away — from banks, brokerage houses, investment companies. If you have been using the services of a tax accountant, request copies of tax returns for the past several years. Don't overlook hidden assets, such as your husband's pension. In most states, pensions are now considered marital property and are subject to division by the court.

Decide what your goals and priorities are before setting up a budget.

House Rich, Cash Poor

The condition of being house rich and cash poor is not uncommon among women who find themselves on their own in midlife. If you are a homeowner and your present financial resources are inadequate for your needs, you may have to balance the present against the future by taking out a loan against your house or by selling your house and investing the money from the sale. You might also consider selling your house to one of your children — with a proviso that assures you of lifetime occupancy with monthly payments to you against the selling price.

If you have enough equity in the house to qualify for a new mortgage and if current rates are substantially lower than your mortgage rate, it might be to your advantage to refinance the loan. This can improve your cash flow, reduce your income-tax payments, and save you many thousands of dollars.

Make a careful assessment of the costs involved, and weigh them against the reduced interest rate. Make sure your total costs are lowered and that you are not just shifting costs around.

Before refinancing your mortgage, consider the following: How long do you plan to stay in your present house? If you plan to stay longer than a year, refinancing may be worthwhile, depending on your mortgage rate and rates available.

MONEY SCAMS

Midlife women who have been divorced or widowed and have had little or no experience in money management are especially vulnerable to financial con artists. A widow in her late 50s who lost $150,000 in a financial-planning scheme described her experience as "a punishment for my ignorance and gullibility. After my husband died, I was looking for investments that would give me enough income to live on. Instead, it all went down the drain and I had to go back to work to support myself."

In a similar case, a 58-year-old woman lost her entire life savings of $165,000 when a shyster representing himself as a financial planner defrauded hundreds of investors out of more than $10 million. The woman, who suffers from arthritis, is unable to work and was forced to move in with her married daughter.

Get-rich-quick schemes that offer to double or triple the value of your investments in a short period have a seductive appeal for women who are on their own and are seeking financial security. But with financial fraud on the rise in recent years, you should be on the alert and aware of possible traps and pitfalls before buying into any investment program.

These are some warning signs to watch out for:

❖ A telephone call from a broker offering to sell you penny stocks, stocks that sell for a few cents or a few dollars each. You must decide by tonight, before the stocks double. Penny-stock scams have cost the public hundreds of millions of dollars a year, reported *Business Week*.

❖ You are offered an "investment opportunity" in which the returns are substantially higher than average. A rate of 5 percent to 10 percent above Treasury rates should raise the warning flags.

❖ Be wary of offers from companies who are headquartered in the Bahamas or Tahiti or other offshore locations because of the tax advantages. Lax disclosure requirements make it next to impossible to get reliable financial information from these companies, and you can expect no help from government agencies. Some offshore companies are legitimate, but many are run by con artists.

❖ When someone makes you an offer by telephone that sounds interesting, ask for a prospectus with a detailed analysis of the deal. Never send a deposit or give out a valid credit card number without a careful study of the prospectus.

❖ Research the company. Look into its history and the credentials of its officers. Check it out with government agencies, such as the Securities and Exchange Commission.

❖ Before making a substantial investment, consult the experts. Talk to your accountant, financial counselor, or attorney. The fees for these services may be the best investment you can make, if they keep you out of the clutches of financial con artists.

MONEY IN THE FAMILY

Let's say you've set up a budget that takes care of your present needs and those of the foreseeable future. Your children are on their own, so you can now settle back and enjoy these rich, fruitful years. What's wrong with this picture? There may be nothing wrong with it; in fact, it is a scenario of midlife as you can and should experience it.

But your carefully structured program for managing money can be thrown into disarray by the kind of family crises that, as we've seen, tend to erupt at this time of our lives. The pressures of the sandwich generation are often money-related. When an adult child moves back home, household expenses increase. Adult children may require financial assistance to tide them over a personal or career problem. An aging parent's illness can be a financial as well as an emotional drain.

Family problems like these are unpredictable, and yet they should have a place in your financial planning. A portion of your earned income or assets should be set aside to take care of such emergencies. Your parents and children should also be allocating part of their income from earnings or other sources into an emergency fund.

Family money problems become more manageable when family finances are discussed honestly and openly. When I was researching parent–adult children relationships for my book *Once My Child, Now My Friend,* I learned that in many families, like the one I grew up in, money is a hush-hush subject. "The veil of silence that is drawn over the topic," I wrote, "serves as a cover for the anxiety and ambivalence in which family finances become enveloped, especially in middle-income families."

Aging parents often want to keep their money problems under wraps to spare their children, who, they are quick to assert, "have their own problems." But ignorance about their parents' financial affairs makes it more difficult for the children to deal with crises when they arise. A 48-year-old woman whose father had a massive coronary attack was shocked to find that her mother knew nothing at all about their finances. "She was helpless. She had never paid a bill or made out a tax return. I had to take care of everything, working mostly in the dark because my mother didn't know where the records were. Fortunately, my father recovered, but it was an unnerving experience."

Make sure that you and your siblings, if you have any, are fully informed about your parents' finances. Discuss with your parents the importance of keeping clear records, and have them give you an updated listing of insurance policies, bank-books, loan and mortgage documents, and any other relevant financial papers. If one or both parents are working, you should know about their company's pension and health insurance program.

On the other side of the sandwich, an adult child's request for financial assistance can push more emotional buttons than an aging parent's money problems. The responsibility for our children weighs more heavily on us. How can we refuse them when they are in need? What will our refusal do to our relationship?

In today's economy, the midlife woman who has a high-salaried job or a successful business is likely to be in better financial circumstances than her children, who may not be able to buy a house or a car at today's inflated prices. Under these circumstances, turning down a grown child's request for a loan can bring on an acute case of maternal guilt.

But the consensus among parents who have been through this experience is that you are not doing your adult children a favor by subsidizing them, and you are putting the relationship at risk by letting your son or daughter revert to a weakened, dependent role. "Ask yourself why you're making the loan," suggests Judy Barber, a San Francisco family therapist. If you're using the money as a means of control and do not expect it to be returned, you would do better to say no to the loan and be honest with your child about the reason for your decision.

Lending money to adult children should be a business transaction between responsible adults. The loan should be put in writing so it is clear that there is an obligation to repay the money. If you prefer not to become involved in a financial transaction with your child, you can arrange for the loan to be handled through your bank, using certificates of deposit or stocks as security. The dual advantage of this approach is that it builds a credit rating for your child and lets you maintain your assets; it also assures you of a foundation on which to structure your retirement plan.

PLANNING FOR THE GOLDEN YEARS

Retirement may be the farthest thing from your mind. You are in your prime, at the peak of your energies. You have come through your midlife crises with renewed vigor. You are enjoying your job and the opportunity to do all the things you never had time for until now. Retirement? That's a hazy prospect, far off in the future. Besides, there's the company pension; that should take care of it.

But in these uncertain times, company pension plans are no longer the solid ground on which you can safely base your retirement strategy. Today, company downsizing forces many older employees into retirement before their pensions have matured. Corporate cost cutting may also include the termination of pensions altogether and the reduction of health benefits. And if, like many women, you have postponed your career until midlife, you cannot expect much if anything from the company's pension plan. In planning for your retirement, you will have to be self-reliant.

The starting point for retirement planning is a question: How do I want to live when my working days are over? If your answer is "I want to continue living as I am now," the rule of thumb is that you will need 70 percent to 80 percent of your preretirement income to maintain your present living standards. This figure is based on the assumption that you will be cutting back on clothes, transportation to and from your job, and other work-related expenses.

But suppose you cannot realistically look forward to this projected level of income, even with social security and a pension. What are your options? You could rent your house or apartment or condominium and move to a less-expensive neighborhood. Or you could retire to a small rural community where the cost of living would be considerably lower due to the lack of economic opportunities. Retirees who have made this choice are enthusiastic about the peace and quiet, the neighborliness, and the lack of crime.

Mapping out a retirement plan brings the present and the future together, a perspective on time that is important for midlife women who, if they have been full-time homemakers, often find it difficult to think about the future. The dailiness of keeping house and raising children tends to shrink the sense of time to the here and now so that anything beyond the day after tomorrow appears hazy and unreal. Although there is no clear crystal ball to reveal the shape of the future, the planning you do today with the resources now available to you can ward off some of the risks and hazards of the later years.

Thinking seriously about tomorrow gives you the impetus to explore and adopt sensible spending, saving, and investment practices today. If, for example, you do not have a retirement tax-break program through your work, you can invest up to $2,000 in an individual retirement account (IRA) without being taxed on the portion of your income that you invest or on the interest accrued. Up to 6 percent of your gross income can be invested tax-deferred.

Your investment program should be guided by conservative principles. Play it safe by putting your money into high-grade securities or mutual funds that offer adequate income together with low risk.

Financial experts tell us that, although we are living longer, most of us are unprepared for retirement and will be facing some unpleasant surprises when we are ready to leave the world of work. This is certainly true for women who are making the transition from financial dependency to control of their financial affairs. But planning for a comfortable retirement is actually no more nor less than an extension of sensible money management into your post-working years.

Today, with advances in health care extending our lives, we can look forward to a longer retirement, which makes planning for those golden years more important than ever before.

BECOMING MONEYWISE

Money management is beginning to lose some of its mystery for midlife women who, because of divorce, widowhood, the needs of aging parents, or other shifting currents, have had to assume financial responsibility for themselves and their families. In addition, career opportunities for women in financial management have been improving and women have been establishing themselves in such formerly male-only fields as banking, investment, and accounting.

In today's complex, fast-changing world, becoming moneywise is essential not only to survival but to personal growth and self-understanding. How you manage your money is a key to your identity as a self-reliant, resourceful, forward-looking woman. Finding a middle ground between needless self-denial and wasteful extravagance is possible only if you are in touch with your real needs and goals and can make independent decisions about your financial affairs. When you are in control of your money, you are in control of your life.

CHAPTER NINE

ঽঙ

Menopause:
The Myths and
the Realities

ঽঙ

NINE

Now, when a few children are sufficient and women have other gratifications in life, relatively few women suffer from notable menopausal problems. Most are pleased to be free of the bother of menstruation and of the possibility of a late, undesired pregnancy.

Theodore Lidz, "The Person"

Like many women of the generation in transition from the premodern era, I went into menopause uninformed and unprepared for it. Since it was never discussed openly among the women in my family, I remained ignorant about this midlife passage until I was well into my teens. From bits of information I picked up here and there, I gathered that women experienced something known as change of life. But exactly what this change was and how it manifested itself was unclear to me, like so much about the female body and its functioning.

One day, when I returned home from school, I found my mother lying in bed, her face flushed, a cold compress on her forehead. My energetic, bustling mother in bed in the middle of the day? This was clearly a cause for worry. I urged her to call the doctor, something we did in our family only in life-and-death emergencies. She shook her head. All my pleas met with the same response: There was nothing a doctor could do for her.

Finally she said in an embarrassed whisper, "It's woman's trouble." And for the first time in our lives, she broke the taboo and talked to me about this hush-hush subject: this sickness, as she called it, that came to women when they were no longer able to bear children. As she described the symptoms — the hot flashes, the sweating, the weakness — it became obvious that for her, this change was the beginning of the end, leaving nothing to look forward to except the desolation of old age.

Years later, when she talked more freely about her past, I learned that her physical discomforts during her menopause had actually been mild and that it was her fears, her anxieties, all that she had been led to expect and dread that had taken their toll, sapping her energy and bringing on symptoms of illness. As a young woman, she had been a beauty, and a future in which she would be without her youthful appeal was a bleak prospect. When she was in her 50s, my father left her for a younger woman; she was convinced that her fears had been realized and that, in her menopause, she had been deprived of all that gave her value as a woman — her reproductive function and her role as a wife.

Despite today's openness about female sexuality, there are many bright, educated, and sexually sophisticated women whose ideas about menopause are hazy and confused. In surveys conducted during the past two decades, women in their late 30s and early 40s admitted that their fears of menopause were based on the unpleasant physical and emotional symptoms associated with it and on their perception of it as youth's biological swan song. In fact, as I discovered in my interviews, younger women often have a more negative view of this midlife transition than many women who are going through it or are postmenopausal.

PRISONERS OF THE BODY

Throughout history, menstruation and menopause, the biological boundaries marking off women's reproductive function have been viewed as dangerously unstable passages affecting women's minds as much as their bodies. The ancients believed that a menstruating woman could turn beer sour, spoil milk and wine, and cause pregnant mares to miscarry. In literature, the menopausal woman is moody, erratic, and dangerously unbalanced. She is Chaucer's wife of Bath, Shakespeare's Lady Macbeth, O'Neill's Mary Tyrone in *Long Day's Journey into Night*, Edith Wharton's Zenobia, the withdrawn, melancholy wife of Ethan Frome.

Even today, despite our uninhibited attitude toward sex, remnants of the old mysteries and taboos linger, preserving the myth of menstruation and menopause as synonymous with mental illness. In the early 1980s, a U.S. district judge made light of a sex-discrimination suit, saying that "Women have a monthly problem which upsets them emotionally, and we all know that."

Until recently, reliable information about menopause was virtually nonexistent. In the past, many women died before going into menopause — the life expectancy of a female infant in 1890 was 44.5 years. And since this "change of life" portended so many dire symptoms, it was rarely discussed, even among women. There is hardly any mention of it in 18th- or 19th-century women's writings — diaries, letters, journals, books. Whatever knowledge there was came mainly from male sources, which, reflecting male biases, added to the myths and misinformation on the subject.

In the past, the perception of menopausal women as victims of their "raging hormones" meant that a woman who was suffering from an actual illness at this time of her life — digestive problems, a kidney ailment, cancer — might not receive the care she needed since her symptoms were often ascribed to menopause. These attitudes were part of a general pre-20th-century perception of women as prisoners of their bodies, while men were thought to be governed by their minds. It followed that women's bodily functions, in particular menstruation and menopause, were mysterious, uncontrollable, and unpredictable, whereas men's bodies were regulated by clear, logical principles which could be applied by medical science.

In the latter part of the 19th century, as medicine became professionalized and developed specialties, the study and treatment of menopause and other women's "diseases" began attracting medical research in America and Western Europe. The preponderantly male medical profession busied itself gathering data, formulating various theories to demystify menopause, and writing sex and marriage manuals that included the latest "scientific" information on menopause.

One of the most popular of these publications was G. H. Naphey's *Physical Life of a Woman: Advice to the Maiden, Wife and Mother*, published in 1871, which offered a profile of the menopausal woman as "depressed, fretful, peevish, annoying to all those around her, impossible to live with." Her symptoms included "a sense of choking, a feeling of faintness, shooting pains in the back and limbs, creepings and chilliness . . ." Her sufferings were part of Mother Nature's plan "to bring about the mysterious transformation in the economy by which she deprives the one sex forever of partaking in the creative act after a certain age, while she only diminishes the power of the other."

A more positive view of menopause surfaced as women began entering the medical profession in the late 19th century. Unlike most of their male colleagues, women physicians saw their female patients as complex human beings who were not defined by their reproductive role. From their experience in treating midlife women, they were able to offer reassurance about menopause, presenting it as a time when women, freed from their child-rearing responsibilities, could enjoy a richer and healthier life.

Two important developments in this century, the discovery of hormones and the growth of the women's health movement, have removed much of the mystery from this stage in women's lives. Yet a few old ideas, stubborn leftovers from the past, are still with us. The most tenacious of these misconceptions is the belief that menopause is a deficiency disease and the idea that it represents the end of a woman's sexual life. Happily, the myths and stereotypes are gradually giving way before ongoing research, the influence of women physicians who are bringing to the practice of medicine a sensitivity to women's health problems, and the real-life experiences of women who are going through menopause.

PREPARING FOR MENOPAUSE: THE REALITIES

Menopause, which means "final menstruation" and is also known as the "climacteric," is a gradual biological process that typically begins between the mid-40s and early 50s, though it has been known to occur as early as 35 and as late as 60. Most women experience some physical changes as their menstrual periods become irregular in frequency and flow. These changes are brought on by a decrease in the frequency of ovulation.

At birth, female infants are equipped with several hundred thousand potential eggs, of which only about four hundred mature. When the period of fertility comes to an end, nature, in the interest of biological economy, shrinks and dries up the ovaries, causing a decline in the production of the two vital female hormones, estrogen and progesterone. During and after menopause the vagina narrows and the lining of the womb atrophies.

The most common physical symptom is the hot flash, which is actually a dilation of the blood vessels; it usually lasts no more than a minute and is harmless. There is no medical consensus on the cause of hot flashes, but a widely accepted theory is that this condition is linked to lowered levels of estrogen. Recommended treatment: Take a cool shower; maintain room temperature at around 68 degrees; wear loose, comfortable garments; and most important, keep a calm and relaxed attitude.

Other typical symptoms are fatigue, moodiness, insomnia, depression. But these reactions to the changes that are taking place in the body vary widely among midlife women from "most difficult time of my life" to "never felt any discomfort." As Sallie Olsen, a San Francisco psychotherapist, emphasizes, "A woman's attitude toward menopause and how much information she has about it make a difference in how she experiences the process."

Recent information about menopause, based on case studies and other research, is revising women's attitudes toward this critical transition. We no longer accept as gospel truth ideas such as these:

- ❖ That women in menopause are more likely to be depressed than other women. Depression in midlife may be due to any number of complex emotional and physical factors that are unrelated to menopause itself. Although hormonal change has a role in depression, it can now be controlled with hormone replacement therapy.

- ❖ That women's interest in sex declines with the onset of menopause. In fact, many women become more sexually responsive with the lessening of their domestic burdens and responsibilities.

EASING INTO MENOPAUSE

Despite all we have learned about menopause, it is still not possible to predict the exact age of its arrival. Though researchers have considered various predictors — age when menstruation begins, use of birth-control pills, hereditary factors —

the age range has remained constant over time — between 48 and 52, the median age continuing at 51. But even without a precise timetable, women can prepare themselves for menopause; the mid-30s are not too early to begin developing the psychological and physical resources that will ease their way through this midlife transition.

The best preparation is an active, healthy life, a positive attitude toward menopause, and supportive personal and family relationships. Women who feel secure about themselves and their marriage and family life report fewer symptoms than those who are having marital problems or difficulties with their children. There is also some evidence of a correlation between education levels, job satisfaction, and menopausal symptoms. Women with satisfying careers that require a high level of education have an easier transition through the climacteric than women who have had less education and are working at menial jobs.

Guidelines for easing into menopause:

❖ A healthy diet is a top priority. Cut back on saturated fats and cholesterol. Limit saturated fats — found in meat, oils, cream, eggs, butter, and other dairy products — to less than 10 percent of your daily caloric intake. A diet of calcium-rich foods can help prevent bone loss.

❖ Follow a program of exercise. The recommended schedule is at least three times a week. Regular aerobic exercise improves muscle strength, keeps cholesterol levels in check, and lowers blood pressure.

❖ If you smoke, quit. Smokers tend to experience more menopausal symptoms than nonsmokers and are at greater risk of developing heart disease.

❖ Take careful inventory of the stress factors in your life and make a determined effort to eliminate as many as possible. This may mean a change of job or ending a stressful relationship, which can ease the way not only through menopause but through other aspects of the midlife passage as well.

❖ Learn all you can about the therapeutic approaches to menopause so that when the time comes, you will be able to make informed decisions, in cooperation with your doctor, about the care and treatment that best suits your needs.

❖ Realize that menopause cannot be separated from the personal, family, and career changes that ordinarily occur in midlife but should be considered within the totality of your health and life experience. The time of life when a woman becomes menopausal is a time of other major changes, so the emotional difficulties that are brought on by the problems and pressures of this midlife passage are often mistakenly attributed to menopause.

VARIETIES OF MENOPAUSAL EXPERIENCE

Each woman's experience of menopause is unique. The following stories make it clear that menopause does not lend itself to easy classification and must be treated on an individualized basis.

The Awakening of a Sleeping Princess

The loss of youth and the fear of declining sexual attractiveness can be traumatic for women whose self-image has been based on their physical appeal. In *The Second Sex*, Simone de Beauvoir commented that women who think they have no other resources than their physical charms will wage a lifetime battle to preserve them.

A woman who could have inspired de Beauvoir's comment is Laurie D., who is approaching her 49th birthday. As the beauty of her family, her striking good looks — cornsilk hair; creamy skin; delicate features; a slender, shapely body — have been the source of her self-definition and emotional security. Pampered and petted in childhood by her parents, envied by women and pursued by men, she is now in her third marriage, the wife of a wealthy businessman for whom she is a showpiece and the lodestar in his universe.

Free from the necessity of earning a living and with her family and household responsibilities in the hands of a competent domestic staff, she has been able to spend much of her time preserving her two most valuable assets — her face and figure. Her time has been taken up with exercise classes, shopping for clothes and cosmetics, having her hair done, and recently, a few discreet tucks in the lines around her eyes and mouth. And of course, her husband's business, which was international finance, involves them in a steady round of social activities.

If you had asked her whether she was a happy, fulfilled woman, she would have answered "Yes, of course." What else could she ask of life? Oh, now and then, there were a few nagging doubts, a sense of inner emptiness, but these existential twitches never lasted more than a moment or two. She could dispatch them quickly by having her hair done or planning a dinner party.

Last year, when her menopause began, she was jolted into a sudden, terrifying awareness of what lay ahead. All she could see was a bleak and barren future in which she would be without the supporting props of youth and beauty and the sexual power that went with these endowments.

She sank into a depression that was, in her description, "like drowning in a dark and bottomless pool. My doctor said it was menopause and I'd get over it. But I was scared, so scared I could hardly get through each day. I'd always thought that menopause meant the end of a woman's sex life, so I withdrew from my husband, turned cold on him. When he wanted sex, I wasn't in the mood, and when he insisted, well, he could as well have been making love to a block of ice.

"I don't know what kept the marriage going, except that for both of us, it was important for appearances—for our family and our friends and for the kind of life we were living. Then what happened was—I fell in love—with my exercise instructor, a young guy, no more than 30, with a body that a Greek god could envy. I know now it wasn't really love, it was just good old sex. For me, it was like—you know that story about the sleeping princess who wakes up when the prince kisses her? That's how it was—I woke up, and realized I was still sexy and could still enjoy it.

"It didn't last. These things never do when there's nothing else in it except the physical part. But it probably saved my marriage. My husband doesn't know what happened. Maybe one of these days, I'll tell him. I don't think he'll care. He's so happy we're back to the way we were. And our sex life is better than ever.

"But I realize now that nothing lasts. I used to think I'd always be young and attractive and sexy. I never thought about tomorrow. Now I think about it. I think about making some changes in my life. I don't know what it's going to be, but I know I've got to put my life on some kind of track. And I'll do it. I'm not sure how, but I'll do it."

When Biological Clocks Collide

With women marrying and having babies in their 30s and 40s, a new type of tension has developed on the midlife scene between the teenage girl who is starting to menstruate and her mother who is entering menopause. Dana M., 50 years old, is a free-lance industrial designer who has been married for 22 years to an advertising executive. She is also the mother of 13-year-old Melissa. Dana postponed childbearing until she had established herself in her career. She had her last menstrual period six months ago.

As she describes it, "I expected to take menopause in my stride, never had a moment's worry about it. I was glad to be rid of the monthly bother. What I hadn't counted on was Melissa's adolescence breaking out at the same time. She had a few PMS symptoms, nothing earth-shaking, but she was doing the whole teenage number — smoking pot, hanging out with some real disreputable types. I worried about her getting pregnant. You hear so much about that these days. It's so different from when I was her age. Sex wasn't a casual, fun thing. It was serious. It was a commitment.

"I'd never been depressed before, but now it was like living under a dark cloud. I was restless, irritable, couldn't work, could hardly function at all. Melissa and I were always at each other. I began having hot flashes. I was always tired. I thought, 'So this is what menopause is like.' It began affecting my marriage. Ben, my husband, said he'd had it with our raging hormones; if things went on this way, he was walking out. So I went into therapy. My therapist agreed my problem was menopause. She said maybe I should try estrogen replacement. But I'd heard estrogen could be risky, so I decided to let it go.

"And then Melissa got interested in music, started playing the guitar, then switched to the violin. You wouldn't believe the change in her. She plays in the school orchestra and she's thinking seriously about a musical career. Things are getting better between us now, occasional little disagreements, but nothing out of the ordinary. And my depression and all my other symptoms — they're gone. Maybe it was the timing, my biological clock and Melissa's going off at the same time."

Beating the Clock

The message from nature's time machine — that the reproductive stage of life is coming to an end — often brings on a desire to beat the clock and become pregnant one last time. This belated yearning for a child is most acute in women who, in the early stages of the midlife transition, still have traditional ideas about motherhood. Here is Carol H., 48 years old, a volunteer at a nursing home. She's been married for 28 years to an aerospace engineer:

"My menopause started about two years ago, soon after the youngest of my three sons left for college. I was ready for it, or at least I thought I was. But when my periods became irregular and I knew this was it, a feeling came over me like a hunger that could be satisfied only by having another child before it was too late. It was crazy, but it was like I was possessed. Sure, the house seemed empty at first with the boys gone. But I was getting used to that, and there were moments when I really appreciated the peace and quiet. I don't know how to explain it, except I just couldn't bear to let that door close on me.

"I had dreams about babies. When I saw women with their babies on the street or in the supermarket, I envied them. I couldn't think about anything else except this need, this desire for a child.

"I knew better than to talk about my feelings to Rob, my husband. He would have had me committed. Rob is 15 years older than me, and he had already started talking about early retirement. So I didn't tell him I'd quit taking the pill. But when my periods stopped, I wasn't sure — was it menopause or was I really pregnant? My gynecologist gave me the answer. She told me I was in my third month. That was a real zinger. Made me feel like I'd won first prize in a lottery. I'd beaten the odds and proved I could still create life. The doctor's warnings about having a baby late in life passed right by me. I was on a high, up there on cloud nine, and nothing was going to bring me down.

"When I told Rob, it was what I expected. He nearly went through the roof. He said this was ruining all his plans. He'd been looking forward to retiring in a few years, taking it easy, doing some traveling. Now that was all down the drain. He said I'd tricked him. He said things to me I wouldn't have believed would ever come out of his mouth. Then he got sort of resigned and even made some encouraging noises, like 'OK, if that's the way it is, let's make the best of it.'

"I was going into my fourth month, and I'd had all these tests showing that everything was OK with the baby, or the fetus, as they called it. They could even tell it was female. I'd always wanted a daughter, and so did Rob, so that gave us a lift. Then I woke up one night with the most god-awful cramps, and I was hemorrhaging. So Rob rushed me to the hospital, and they did what they could, but it wasn't any use. I lost the baby. My doctor told me it wasn't unusual for a woman my age to miscarry. She threw a lot of technical terms at me and said I should look on the bright side — how would I like having to deal with an adolescent when I was in my 60s? Something to think about, I had to admit.

"After I got over being depressed about my loss, menopause was a breeze. I came through it, physically and mentally, feeling better than ever before. It's hard for me now to believe I was so desperate about having another child. Menopausal madness, Rob calls it. I don't know. I'm thinking maybe it's got something to do with the way we make such a big deal about motherhood, making women feel that unless they can have babies, they're not worth much. If we can get rid of that kind of thinking, women won't have so many problems with menopause."

Changing the Motherhood-Menopausal Connection

The menopausal experience that has been most painful for women in the past has been confronting the end of motherhood. But women's fear of being devalued when their reproductive years are over is becoming less acute as more realistic perceptions of motherhood are challenging the romanticized attitudes of the past. In her 1981 study of the maternal instinct, *The Myth of Motherhood*, sociologist Elisabeth Badinter reports that women are feeling more keenly the duality and conflict between their maternal "inside" role centered on the home and their worldly feminine role directed toward the "outside." More and more women, she observes, are cutting down on household and maternal activities and no longer consider the home as their natural realm.

For women today, motherhood is an option, not an absolute requirement. It is a stage in their lives, not a lifetime role. Being a mother is no longer enough to give women a firm sense of who they are. Feminine identity is a complex blend of many influences, relationships, achievements, and developmental factors that integrate the reproductive function but are not dependent upon it. Women's changing attitude toward the maternal role is easing and even eliminating problems that develop during menopause but are actually produced by the empty-nest syndrome.

CARE AND TREATMENT

Today, women have a number of options available to them for the care and treatment of menopausal symptoms. "A woman approaching menopause should give serious thought to her options whether she has symptoms or not," advises Dr. Lidia Rubinstein, an obstetrician-gynecologist and associate clinical professor at the University of California, Los Angeles. "What she decides will influence the rest of her life, not only her health but also her appearance and her behavior."

In her practice, three questions that Dr. Rubinstein hears repeatedly from women who are approaching menopause are When do I start hormone replacement therapy? How long must I use it? Does it increase the risk of cancer?

When doctors disagree about the treatment of menopause, it is usually in regard to hormone replacement therapy (HRT). Since the most common menopausal symptoms—hot flashes, night sweats, vaginal dryness—are associated with falling levels of estrogen, this has been the most popular treatment since the 1940s. In fact, estrogen replacement has been proven effective in controlling hot flashes and night sweats and easing vaginal dryness.

However, since the 1970s, it was discovered that high doses of estrogen appeared to increase the risk of uterine cancer, and questions have arisen recently about a possible risk of breast cancer. As a result, the medical profession has been taking a more cautious attitude toward HRT. Although some doctors still believe that estrogen replacement is the menopausal therapy closest to a fountain of youth, others are wary of the risks and prescribe it only in extreme cases.

To reduce the risk of uterine cancer, doctors today prescribe estrogen together with progestin, a synthetic form of the hormone progesterone. A recent study showed a decrease in uterine and ovarian cancer among women using combined HRT. Studies also indicate that heart attacks, which increase after menopause, are reduced by 50 percent with the use of HRT.

Obviously, more research is needed before HRT is accepted as a cure for the common symptoms of the climacteric. Meanwhile, women who are considering estrogen replacement are advised to weigh the risks against the benefits and to investigate alternative forms of care and treatment that have been proven safe and effective.

ALTERNATIVE APPROACHES

Specialists such as Dr. Peter Schmidt, chief of the Reproductive Endocrine Studies Unit of the National Institute of Mental Health, are exploring new approaches to the care and treatment of menopausal symptoms. "People have spent a lot of time investigating what the menopause isn't," Dr. Schmidt maintains, "and I think it's time that we open our eyes more and look at what's actually there." Dr. Schmidt has established a menopause clinic for the study of hormone levels and behavior and mood swings in premenopausal and menopausal women.

Clinics specializing in the care and treatment of menopause have been appearing around the country. They provide information and support not usually offered by the medical establishment, particularly as medicine has become increasingly depersonalized. The clinics offer a variety of activities designed to help women overcome their anxieties and develop confidence in their ability to cope with their menopausal problems. In the clinic operated by the University of California's San Diego campus, women attend a half-day session in which they are given the basic information they need to make their decisions about their own therapy. The clinic also operates a "hot-flash line" that women can call when they need information or emotional support.

At a clinic in Florida, women receive a complete physical, mammogram, cholesterol profile, bone-density measurement, and an exercise stress test. An evaluation of muscle strength serves as a guide to prescribing an exercise program based on the women's individual needs. If, for example, a woman has been leading a sedentary life, she might spend some time on resistance-training machines before beginning regular aerobic exercise as a means of avoiding painful joints. Specialists at the clinic include physicians, a psychologist, a nutritionist, a physical therapist, and an exercise physiologist.

Clinics that offer one-stop comprehensive services are undoubtedly on the wave of the future in women's health care. But since they are still few and far between, most women who are seeking help during the menopause must shop around for the services they need. But if they have educated themselves and can separate knowledge from myth, they should be able to organize a comprehensive health program that is suited to their individual needs. With more varied information and resources for treating menopause on the increase, and more effective care and treatment becoming available, women can look forward to a smoother transition to what anthropologist Margaret Mead has referred to as "postmenopausal zest."

A WELCOME CHANGE

As menopause casts off the negative myths and stereotypes of the past, it is being seen in a new light, as a passage to freedom and independence. In a recent survey of women in their 50s, the majority of the participants described menopause as a relief. The psychologists who conducted the survey, Valory Mitchell of the California School of Professional Psychology and Ravenna Helson of the University of California at Berkeley, found that most of the women surveyed considered menopause a welcome change which ended worries about pregnancy and birth control and put an end to a monthly nuisance.

This positive attitude toward menopause reflects the changing image and role of the midlife woman. No longer limited to her biological role, and with an expanded range of options available to her for smoothing the way through the menopausal passage, she can be free to control her body instead of being controlled by it. She can discover that the change of life is a change for the better.

 za

Healthwise Women

za

TEN

Learning to understand, accept, and be responsible for our physical selves, we can start to use our untapped energies. Our image of ourselves is on a firmer base, we can be better friends and better lovers, better people, more self-confident, more autonomous, stronger and more whole.

<u>Our Bodies, Ourselves</u>, Boston Women's Health Collective

Sometime during my 50s, I stopped taking my health for granted. Until then, I had assumed that the good health I had always enjoyed was an inalienable right, my natural heritage, as much a part of me as the color of my eyes. I had sailed through menopause without missing a beat in my busy, demanding work and family schedules. The pressures of the generational sandwich and the pangs of empty-nesthood, whatever their emotional costs, had not affected my state of physical well-being. Though I ate what I pleased, indulging my sweet tooth whenever possible, and avoided all exercise except for an occasional walk on the beach, my weight remained stable. When I made my annual visit to my doctor for a routine checkup, his pronouncement was always the same: "Everything's fine."

What was it that made me aware of my body's vulnerability at a time when I had resolved most of my midlife family problems and was on the brink of a new career, looking forward to a future that seemed full of exciting possibilities? It was not a major event, no serious illness or accident, but rather a succession of small, subtle signals. I noticed that I tired more easily and needed more sleep to get me through the day. A sudden weight gain required letting out seams in most of my wardrobe. This "too too solid flesh" was beginning to show signs of sagging here and there. My doctor, instead of his usual "All's well" report, warned me that my cholesterol level was dangerously high and put me on a rigorous diet. Meanwhile, I kept hearing about mutual friends, acquaintances, and relatives, women close to my age, who had suffered a heart attack, been diagnosed as diabetic, discovered they had cancer of the breast or cervix, or recently undergone a hysterectomy.

It gradually dawned on me that I could not go on blithely ignoring the changes occurring in my body and expect to feel as buoyantly healthy as I did in my youth. I would have to abandon my laissez-faire attitude and begin taking responsibility for my health, which, despite my good record, obviously did not come with a lifetime guarantee. If I wanted to make the most of these years, I would have to be on the alert for the special health problems of this time of life.

I realized that the promise of the middle years, the opportunities for growth and self-renewal, are dependent on our maintaining a healthy mind in a healthy body. This means that we must stay in touch with our physical and psychological needs and be aware of the health-care resources that are available to us today.

HEALTH CARE OR MEDICAL CARE?

The Information Gap

Until recently, there has been an information gap in the area of health care for middle-aged women. Research funded by the government has targeted mainly male-related health issues. Research and treatment of women have focused on their reproductive system to the exclusion of such social and psychological influences as marital status, relationships with children and parents, and career problems, factors which have been included in most male-related studies.

The good news is that women's health problems are coming to the forefront of medical research. The federal government is engaged in a major study of women's health problems with hundreds of thousands of women participating. The study is expected to cost $500 million and to extend over a period of 10 years.

The project will examine the major causes of illness and death in women, including cancer, heart disease, and osteoporosis, and how these illnesses are affected by menopause and by diet, exercise, hormone replacement therapy, and the cessation of smoking. "Women have a right to know how they can prevent and ameliorate the health problems attendant to growing older," states Dr. Bernardine Healy, director of the National Institutes of Health and the guiding force behind this ground-breaking research effort. Her efforts have been given added impetus by the increase in women's life expectancy and by the growing number of women over 40 in the work force; as midlife women have become more visible and more prominent, their health has become an issue of social and economic significance.

Patricia Schroeder, the Colorado congresswoman who has been a steadfast supporter of increased research into women's health, told the Senate Labor and Human Resources Subcommittee during a discussion of the proposed research project that the lack of information about aging and its relation to women's health has perpetuated the notion that "in our society, men age and women rot." Adding that women pay a price for the inattention to their health problems, many of which begin in midlife, Senator Brock Adams, chairman of the subcommittee, observed that "Women will continue to be at unnecessary risk until the study of the health concerns of midlife and older women become a top priority in the United States."

The Clinical View

Meanwhile, until there is a radical reordering of our priorities in this area, our health-care system will continue to be subject to a set of clinically oriented principles that have been the gospel of mainstream medicine:

- ❖ The human being is a collection of parts to be repaired or replaced.
- ❖ The doctor is an expert, an unchallengeable authority figure.
- ❖ Surgery and technology have high priority.
- ❖ Disease is a static, fixed, intrusive entity.
- ❖ Health problems exemplify a cause-effect relationship.
- ❖ Diagnosis and treatment are approached as scientific abstractions, unaffected by individual or social factors.

A system like this is obviously not capable of dealing with the complex health problems of midlife women. "There is in reality no 'health-care system,'" asserts Catherine DeLorey of the Women's Health Research Institute in Boston, "but rather a 'medical-care system' which by definition perceives life in medical terms. This system, bounded by societally and culturally imposed ideas of women's roles, relies on myths and stereotypes to govern the way health care is provided for women."

In middle age, more so than at any other time in their lives, women's health care must be viewed from the perspective of their changing roles and responsibilities. But in a system that is clinically oriented, the midlife woman is treated as if she were dependent on and controlled by her endocrine system. This simplifies the approach to her health problems: She is given estrogen to control hot flashes or prevent osteoporosis (thinning of the bones) or to ameliorate whatever her problem may be on the assumption that, when her hormonal balance is restored, all will be well.

The clinical approach, with its emphasis on surgery and medication, has serious built-in risks for midlife women. In *Women's Health Alert*, published by the Public Citizen Health Research Group, Dr. Sidney Wolfe comments on "this inexhaustible capacity to cut and medicate women in this country," which he attributes, in part, to "a cultural view that women's natural biological processes are treatable illnesses." It is this cultural view that, Dr. Wolfe charges, is responsible for "millions of unnecessary hysterectomies, surgically delivering 'perfect babies' through cesarean sections, and deforming women's breasts by implanting silicone devices inside their bodies."

Whose Body Is It?

The clinical perspective has another unfortunate aspect: It induces in women a passive attitude toward their health needs. Whereas in former times, women were actively involved in their own and their families' health problems, today we have turned over this responsibility to a depersonalized medical establishment. Because of our reproductive function, we have been made to feel that our bodies, as the bearers and nurturers of human life, are public property.

Throughout history, a woman's body has belonged to her husband, her family, her country. The abortion issue has made us realize that there is still a large area of controversy over the question "Whose body is it?" This "My body, not myself" attitude, which has been imposed on women by society at large and reinforced by the medical profession, has been felt most keenly by women in their middle years who are in their postmotherhood transition. During the childbearing, child-rearing years, we unquestioningly accept Freud's statement that "biology is destiny." From puberty onward, a woman's major decisions are determined by biological and social forces that direct her toward one objective: childbearing. When her reproductive function is behind her, she feels as though her body is no longer of any value. In an effort to conform to a culture that is fixated on youth and slimness, she subordinates all else to the goal of achieving and maintaining a youthful body, a goal for which she will even put her health at risk by excessive dieting.

But women are becoming healthwise and are questioning the cultural imperatives that have led them to risk their health for a superficial ideal of youthful beauty. There is also a growing recognition among women of the need to be fully informed about the more serious midlife health problems and the options for prevention and treatment that can reduce the risks.

MIDLIFE HEALTH RISKS

Breast Cancer

One of the most serious health risks for midlife women is breast cancer. According to present figures, one in nine women is afflicted with this life-threatening illness, and 50 percent of all women will at some point in their life face the problem of a lump in the breast. The discovery can be traumatic, and when the lump is cancerous, even after a complete recovery, women testify that their lives are never again the same as before.

"It changed my life" is how environmental activist Ellen Stern Harris describes her experience with breast cancer. Harris, who has been honored nationally for her longstanding record of service, was 59 when she learned that she had breast cancer, and the trauma has had a profound effect on her self-image and her way of life. "I had always thought of myself as indestructible, as someone with unlimited energy," she told me, "someone who could take on the most difficult challenges and see them through. It took breast cancer to make me realize that I am vulnerable and that I must conserve my time and energies. Now I put limits on the amount of strain I will take. I recently resigned from the board of directors of an organization because there were too many toxic personalities on the board and it was causing me too much stress."

There was a strong genetic factor in her case. "My grandmother had a double mastectomy, and when the mammogram showed two tumorous sites, which had not been detected by the doctors — there was a third one that didn't show up on the mammogram — I was fairly sure I'd have to have a mastectomy. When I consulted two specialists, they agreed that it was the only safe procedure for me."

She has not had breast reconstruction because of the danger that a new cancerous tumor might be concealed underneath. "This happened to a friend of mine," she says, "and I believe it caused her death. It's more important to stay alive than to have a perfect body." She urges women who have had a mastectomy to exercise the arm on the side where the breast has been removed since the surgery often extends to the underarm tissues. "When I'm in the shower, I walk my fingers up the wall, and I make it a point to use that arm in every possible way."

Like Ellen Stern Harris, women today are talking more freely about their experiences with breast cancer. Now that this once hush-hush subject has come out of the closet, women are becoming alerted to the risks of this health problem and the available preventive measures and treatments.

The main risk factors are aging (the risk rises after 50), genetics, and possibly diet. In 15 percent to 20 percent of breast cancer cases, genetics plays a significant part. A woman whose mother or grandmother had breast cancer should be on the alert for any suspicion of a lump in her breast. The role of nutrition is being investigated, and many doctors believe that a diet high in cholesterol, saturated fat, and calories increases the risk. In countries where the diet is very lean — Japan and Singapore, for example — the incidence of breast cancer is one-sixth to one-half of the rate in the United States.

The data on estrogen replacement therapy as a preventive treatment is mixed. Some doctors claim that it reduces the risk; others point to studies that show a link between estrogen replacement therapy and an increase in the incidence of breast cancer. Another controversial issue in the medical profession is the risk of silicone-gel breast implants, one of the most popular forms of plastic surgery. Silicone gel has been identified as a carcinogen that has caused highly malignant cancer in laboratory animals. And though doctors disagree, in 1989 the Food and Drug Administration, estimating that 3 million women have breast implants, issued this warning: "FDA has weighed the probable risks and benefits to the public from the use of the silicone-gel–filled breast prosthesis and believes that the studies present evidence of significant risks associated with the use of the device. These risks must be addressed by the manufacturers of this device."

As of now, the manufacturers have shown no signs of heeding this directive, and warnings about the risks are having little effect on the popularity of implants. The constant drumbeat in the media extolling the full-breasted figure has made women believe that breast augmentation is the key to sexiness. The breast is where the maternal and the sexual come together, and when the maternal function declines, the sexual-erotic aspect is enhanced. Some psychologists see the trend toward bigger breasts as a sign that women, established in the work force, now feel secure enough to be fully feminine in their bodies as well as their attitudes and behavior. "Women are essentially rediscovering their femininity" is how market analyst and an-

thropologist John Lowe sees it, "and obviously, breasts emphasize gender differences."

But a woman in her early 50s who has paid dearly for implants with deformed breasts and years of suffering and pain,
believes that women who have their breasts enlarged by implants are being victimized. "I never expected to be part of a
medical experiment," she sighs, "and now I know that's exactly
what I and thousands of other misguided women have been."

In fact, little is known about the causes of breast cancer, and
the only treatment for it is still surgery — mastectomy or lump-
ectomy, depending on the results of the mammogram and other
tests. The medical profession is unanimous on the importance of early detection as the best way to lower the risk of
developing breast cancer. Three screening tests that are recommended for all midlife women, especially those over 50, are self-
examination, manual examination by a trained clinician, and
X-ray mammography. Though none of these is infallible, mammography is successful in detecting tumors 87 percent of the
time. There are two types of mammograms, each with a different purpose: A screening mammogram is used to detect early
breast cancers in women without symptoms, and a diagnostic
mammogram is performed when a woman has a lump in her
breast. Women over 50 are advised to have a mammogram annually, and those with a genetic history of breast cancer should
also have regular clinical examinations.

Osteoporosis

The loss of bone mass (osteoporosis) is another midlife health
problem that has been neglected by medical research until recently. Not until the early 1980s did osteoporosis begin to at-
tract the attention of health-care professionals. Soon the media became interested, and suddenly this longstanding midlife
health problem was lifted out of obscurity and publicized as a
serious threat to women's health.

Osteoporosis is part of the natural process of aging, in which small amounts of bone mass are gradually reabsorbed by the body. Maximum bone mass is reached in the mid-30s, after which bone formation takes place more slowly than bone absorption. As the remaining skeletal structure thins out, it is less able to support body weight and becomes susceptible to fracture.

Bone metabolism is a complex process, and the rate of bone loss varies widely among individuals. Because menopause is associated with declining levels of estrogen, it is generally believed to be a contributory factor. But the effect of estrogen replacement on osteoporosis is an unsettled question. A diet rich in calcium together with regular exercise are also effective in prevention and treatment.

Now that osteoporosis has been given high visibility, women, many of them angry that it has been neglected until now, are developing an intense interest in this midlife health problem. Questions women ask:

❖ *Who is at greatest risk of developing osteoporosis?*

Women who have a family history of osteoporosis, whose ovaries were removed before they were 40, who are hyperthyroid, have kidney disease, or have had abdominal surgery.

❖ *Is smoking a risk factor?*

In a 1985 study, smokers were shown to have a higher rate of bone loss than nonsmokers.

❖ *What precautions should be taken to avoid fractures?*

Most fractures are caused by falls, but lifting heavy loads can also be hazardous. Preventive measures: Wear low-heeled shoes; have your eyesight checked regularly and wear proper glasses if needed; see the doctor for any symptoms of dizziness or unsteadiness; stay off slippery surfaces and rickety ladders; install bathroom safety features and thick, nonskid rugs; avoid putting any undue strain on your back and legs.

❖ *What should a calcium-rich diet include?*

Nonfat milk and yogurt, fish, shellfish, tofu, and dark green vegetables such as kale, collards, and mustard greens.

❖ *What about calcium supplements?*

Since there is some risk in taking calcium supplements on a regular basis, play it safe by consulting your doctor about levels and types of calcium intake that are right for you.

❖ *What is the role of exercise?*

Women who are physically active are less susceptible to fractures than women who lead sedentary lives. Weight-bearing exercise — walking, running, skiing — increases bone mass and improves muscle tone, strength, and agility. When a group of men and women in their mid-50s who were longtime runners were compared with a comparable group of nonexercisers, it was found that the density of the runners' spines was 40 percent higher than that of the sedentary group.

❖ *In addition to diet and exercise, are there any other safe alternatives to estrogen?*

A recently discovered alternative to estrogen in the treatment of postmenopausal osteoporosis is etidronate. The *New England Journal of Medicine* called it a "welcome new option," and studies have shown that, taken over a period of three years, there was a marked increase in spinal bone mass and a decrease in spinal fractures. Further research is needed to establish the long-term effects.

Heart Disease

Government-funded research on heart disease has been concerned mainly with heart-related illness in men, although in the United States, it is the leading cause of death among women. More than 300,000 women over the age of 50 die of heart disease every year. "The problem of osteoporosis is trivial compared to the problems of heart disease in women," wrote

Dr. Robert Marcus in the *Western Journal of Medicine*. Fortunately, growing medical interest in women's cardiovascular problems has stepped up the pace of research and improved the chances of recovery after an attack.

Although men can have heart attacks from young adulthood onward, in women the problem occurs mostly after menopause. Because the changes that occur in women's bodies at this stage appear to put them at greater risk of a heart attack than when they were younger, some doctors believe that the loss of estrogen protection is an underlying cause of this midlife health problem. Estrogen therapy has been credited with lowering cholesterol levels in postmenopausal women, but there are still questions about the link between menopause and cholesterol. Dr. Bruce Stadel of the Food and Drug Administration is a cautious supporter of estrogen therapy, but he admits that "There simply hasn't been any good ongoing surveillance of vascular disease in women to assess the real effects of hormone replacement therapy." But doctors who are committed to estrogen as a heart-disease preventive for postmenopausal women believe that, even if estrogen therapy increases a woman's chances of breast cancer, the risk is outweighed by the benefits.

Whatever the relationship between menopause and heart disease, studies have revealed that the problem is complex and has many causes including aging, genetic predisposition, stress, diet, obesity, high blood pressure, smoking, lack of exercise. Preventive measures, in addition to estrogen replacement, are those that are basic to maintaining good health generally: a low-fat diet, regular exercise, no smoking, avoiding stress, scheduling periodic medical checkups.

MANAGING STRESS

In the catalog of women's midlife health problems, stress is a relative newcomer. Not very long ago, middle age was regarded as a tranquil time for women. Fifty was thought of as the threshold to old age, a time of life when women, with their children grown and their parents long dead, have earned the right to a peaceful, unpressured existence. The popular image of the woman who was no longer young resembled *Whistler's Mother*.

The image and the reality were actually not too far apart in some cases. I can remember women in my family and the families of friends who, in their middle age, spent their days paying visits, playing cards, doing a bit of shopping. Having married young, they were now grandmothers and were not expected at their age to venture beyond the boundaries of this cozy, enclosed world. The idea of stress as a health problem for women of any age would have been considered bizarre. It was men who were exposed to the strains of earning a living; women who worked outside the home usually performed routine, low-level jobs that presumably made no demands upon their nervous systems.

Midlife women who are combining demanding careers with marriage, motherhood, household management, caring for their aging parents, and attempting to maintain some semblance of a personal and social life can be forgiven for occasionally looking back wistfully at that vanished world of their mothers and grandmothers. The lives of those homebound women were narrow, restricted, humdrum, and not always worry-free, but when they reached middle age, they could settle into a calm, leisurely pace.

Today, as we have seen, midlife can be a frenetic time for women, and stress, which has become a buzz word in the medical profession, is now an equal-opportunity health problem, as much of a threat to women as to men. The connection between stress and health is still an open question and one that is being investigated, but there is little doubt in the health-care professions that the connection is a leading contributor to physical and mental illness. In our pressure-cooker world, it is unrealistic to expect to eliminate stress entirely, but we can learn to manage it so that it does not become a serious health risk.

Stress has been defined as the response of the body to harmful and threatening forces in the environment. But it can also be caused by forces within us that drive us to behave in ways that raise our stress level. These internal pressures are present in many midlife business and professional women. Women in their 40s and 50s still have embedded in their consciousness the idea that, as Janey-come-latelies to the business and professional worlds, they must be constantly proving themselves, forever demonstrating that they can take on the toughest challenges and outperform the male competition.

In addition to being superachievers, they must allay any latent guilt feelings by being available to their husbands, their teenage or adult children, and their aging parents and must also be responsible for household management and for maintaining some semblance of a social life. It is not surprising that stress-related illnesses have been on the rise among middle-aged women.

Stress can be brought on by fear, anxiety, loneliness, and by the kind of major life changes that often occur in midlife. The physical response to stress generally involves a chemical reaction in the body—an increase in the production of certain hormones, which raises the heart rate, blood pressure, respiratory rate, and blood-sugar level. Common stress symptoms are headache, stomachache, sleeplessness, chronic fatigue, palpitations.

Managing stress is not simple and in severe cases may require medical and psychiatric help. But if you are experiencing the kind of day-to-day, work-related, family-related stress that is familiar to midlife women, you can reduce your stress level by making some changes in your mental attitude and your lifestyle. As a start, consider the following:

❖ Assess the sources of stress in your life and decide which you can eliminate or reduce. Avoid as much as possible those people in your social circle or your work environment who are anxiety-producers.

❖ If your job is the cause of your stress-related problems and you are unable to make the necessary stress-reducing changes, consider a change of occupation. As we saw in chapter 7, changing jobs in midlife is no longer unusual and can lead to a more satisfying, less stressful career.

❖ Recognize your limitations and take on only what you can comfortably accomplish in the allotted time.

❖ Assign priorities to your tasks and do the important ones first.

❖ You do not have to be a superwife, a superdaughter, or a superfriend in order to feel that you are fulfilling your responsibilities to others. Nor do you have to feel guilty for whatever goes wrong in the lives of your husband, your children, or your parents. Recognizing your limitations means acknowledging that you do not have God-like powers and that there are limits to what you can do for others.

❖ Make time for yourself, for relaxation, and for the things you enjoy doing.

❖ Work off your stress through the kind of exercise you enjoy.

Not all types of stress are harmful, and some stressful activities and emotions are built into the human condition and the kind of lives we lead today. But we can manage the stress we experience on a day-to-day basis so that we can cope with it comfortably and keep it from becoming a threat to our health.

THE BODY BOUNTIFUL

A source of stress for midlife women is the relentless social pressure to be girlishly slim. The message that we begin receiving when we are in our teens is that a slender, shapely body is vital to our self-esteem and our social and sexual success. That thin girls are popular and fat girls are not is impressed upon us early, and it remains fixed in our consciousness. Film director Henry Jaglom has said that "Women, unlike men, are told early on that happiness and success depend on how they look in a bathing suit."

American women have been so imbued with the fear of body fat that they are willing to spend large amounts of time and money fighting every extra ounce of flesh that shows up on the scale. In their fanatical pursuit of thinness, they starve themselves, exercise to exhaustion, and submit their bodies to expensive and risky procedures such as liposuction and stomach tucks. The effort to meet our societal standards of slimness can be so obsessive that it becomes a threat to physical and mental health. Anorexia and bulimia are among the dietary disorders that are often caused by excessive devotion to the ideal of slimness.

In midlife, the struggle to remain thin is complicated by a slowdown of the metabolism, the process by which food is converted into energy. However, gaining a few pounds in middle age does not mean that you are overweight. Individual variations in body build make it difficult to determine precisely when you have crossed the border into obesity. The general guideline is 20 percent over your normal weight. Obesity is considered severe at 40 percent over normal weight.

But again, there is no strict definition of normal weight. Weight tables that focus on figures of weight according to height, omitting age and other physical characteristics, are too limited to be useful. Your most reliable source for this information is your doctor, whose estimate will reflect your build, musculature, metabolism, and other relevant factors.

The health risk of carrying excess weight is determined not only by the numbers on the scale but also by blood pressure, blood sugar, cholesterol level, and distribution of fat. Obesity increases the risk of developing health problems such as high blood pressure, heart disease, diabetes, gallbladder disease, osteoporosis, and respiratory illness. Some of these conditions may have other causes, but overweight makes it more difficult to treat them.

Weight-loss products have been flooding the market for many years, and weight-reducing salons that promise to make you slim overnight have also been proliferating. But though some of these diet products and reducing methods may succeed in taking off pounds, the effect is usually temporary and there are often health risks involved. The safe, sensible way to lose weight is to follow a diet-and-exercise program under medical supervision and to face the fact that, in order to remain at your normal weight, you will probably have to adopt this life-style permanently.

The importance of maintaining the weight that is best for your health cannot be overestimated. But excessive concern with the body's size and proportions is detrimental to the psychological development of women and tends to perpetuate the stereotype of woman-as-body, man-as-mind. The cult of the body belongs to a time when women had few sources of self-esteem beyond their sexual appeal. It is part of an outworn value system that midlife women must put behind them if they are to take full advantage of the opportunities for growth and achievement that are opening up for them today.

TAKING CHARGE OF YOUR HEALTH

A new activism in the women's health movement promises to make the 1990s the decade of women's declaration of health independence. In the 1970s and 1980s, we saw the birth of women's health consciousness with the formation of the Boston Women's Health Collective and the publication of the seminal book *Our Bodies, Ourselves*. The women's health groups that have formed during the past 20 years have been committed mainly to support and education, to helping women overcome the barriers of shame and ignorance that have separated them from their bodies. Through these efforts, midlife women have learned that their health problems, which had been regarded as weakness, hysteria, or hypochondria, were normal manifestations of female biology, a discovery that did wonders for their self-esteem.

The new groups differ from their predecessors in their concentration on breast and ovarian cancer and their greater political activism. In nearly every case, these grass-roots groups have been formed in response to women's experiences with the medical system — a doctor's failure to diagnose a lump or to provide information about treatment choices. The groups' lobbying efforts, which include demonstrations and meetings with Congress, are directed at increased funding for research and better insurance coverage. They are credited with prodding the National Institutes of Health to undertake its massive study of menopause and related health problems.

Some over-50 women in the groups are struggling with their generation's mixed feelings about civil disobedience. "We're more conservative," said Beverly Zakarian, who had ovarian cancer and is the organizer of a New York group called Can Act. "We're mostly not the type to go out and put bloody handprints on a building." But the alarming rise in breast cancer — 175,000 new cases annually — is activating even some of the more conservative advocacy groups as well as some areas of the medical profession.

Women are discovering that taking charge of their health is literally a matter of life or death. Medical disasters such as the thalidomide and Dalkon-shield scandals and growing concerns over unnecessary surgery and the risks of breast implants have brought women to the realization that the practice of medicine can be hazardous to their health. Midlife women, because of the bodily and other changes in their lives, have a special stake in a safe and sound health-care system. In becoming health-wise women, they are helping to make that system more responsible and compassionate.

≈

CHAPTER ELEVEN

Celebrating the New Middle Age

≈

ELEVEN

She was approaching the August of a woman's life, a period which combines reflection and tenderness, when the maturity which is beginning kindles a warmer flame in the eyes, when strength of heart mingles with experience of life and when, in the fullness of its development, the whole being overflows with a wealth of harmony and beauty.

Gustave Flaubert, <u>A Sentimental Education</u>

In his book *A Brief History of Time*, Stephen Hawking wrote that in the theory of relativity, there is no absolute time, but instead, time is relative and is experienced differently by each individual. The idea of absolute time has weighed heavily on women, for whom the passing of the years has held the fearful prospect of loss — loss of youth, beauty, health, sexuality, and of the role that gave them their primary identity, motherhood. In middle age, the loss of the maternal role, though it lightened their responsibilities, drained their lives of meaning and purpose.

The paradox of a woman's life on reaching middle age was summed up neatly by Simone de Beauvoir in *The Second Sex*: "Toward 50, she is in full possession of her powers; she feels she is rich in experience; that is the age at which men attain the highest positions, the most important posts; as for her, she is put into retirement. She has been taught only to devote herself to someone, and nobody wants her devotion any more. Useless, unjustified, she looks forward to the long, unpromising years she has yet to live, and she mutters: 'No one needs me.'"

The world has taken many turns since de Beauvoir wrote those words in 1953, and there have been many changes since then in the lives of middle-aged women. Today, when a woman arrives at the time of her life when she can say, "No one needs me," the likelihood is that she is expressing relief rather than regret. She has gained that precious, irreplaceable dimension — time, time for herself and for all the plans and dreams that had to be shelved until now. She has learned that, though time brings with it some deprivations, it also offers new opportunities for learning and growing. At last she can free the hidden self that, ever since she became aware of herself as female, has been buried beneath layers of conformity to family and social pressures. Now she can search within herself to discover her personal truth.

FREEING THE HIDDEN SELF

In *So You Want to Go Back to School*, a book I coauthored as a guide for middle-aged people who want to continue their education, we wrote: "The need to be part of an active, social environment is as deep-rooted and as vital to human growth as food or love. As soon as infants begin to look around at the world beyond the cradle, they try to shape these fascinating surroundings to their will. They push aside obstacles; they explore and investigate whatever swims into their ken, demanding attention from those around them. If they are consistently shut away from the world of lively, interesting people and events, they soon become listless and apathetic. Children who show no interest in the world around them, who have no desire to impose their will upon it, stir panic in their parents."

When women who are now in midlife were growing up, it was not they but their brothers who were encouraged to become active participants in the larger world. Before the women's movement and the sexual revolution, women were expected to concern themselves with private matters—with family and household and personal adornment. Excluded from the public world, they became increasingly passive, and those who reached middle age were appendages to their families, without an identity of their own.

For the midlife woman, one of the most liberating outcomes of the women's movement has been the freeing of her hidden self. I have heard women in their 40s and 50s say such things as:

"I'm just beginning to know who I am."

"I've always lived for other people—my parents, my husband, my children. There was someone inside me all the time trying to break free; now it's happening and it's a wonderful feeling."

"It's like I'm just starting to come alive, to feel secure with myself."

In a letter to a friend, Edith Wharton wrote that the only cure for growing older is "to make one's center of life inside of one's self, not selfishly or excludingly, but with a kind of unassailable serenity—to decorate one's inner house so richly that one is content there, glad to welcome anyone who wants to come and stay, but happy all the same in the hours when one is inevitably alone."

The sense of inwardness that Wharton is referring to is rarely achieved in youth, when we are struggling to understand and adapt to the external world. As young women, the social pressures to be popular, to be sexually appealing can be so overwhelming that they keep us from turning to our inner sources of self-understanding and enrichment. Midlife is the most opportune time to discover who we are, to make sense of where we have been as a guide to where we are going. Here, at the midpoint of our lives, we can begin to see a pattern in our experience and development, and it is still open-ended. There is time to make changes, to direct or redirect the course we have been following, even to set out on an entirely new trail.

WHAT DOES IT MEAN TO BE MIDDLE-AGED?

Middle age is an undiscovered terrain in the life span that has no easily discernible boundaries. When does it begin? When does it end? What does it mean to be middle-aged? How can we make these years the best time of our lives? Women in the age range of 45 to 60 offered the following responses to questions like these:

❖ Middle age begins when you stop living in the future and aren't ready to live in the past. You're living in the present and appreciating every moment.

❖ Middle age ends when you're spending more time revisiting the past than enjoying the present and the future seems like a mirage.

❖ When you reach middle age, you become aware of how precious time is, and you are careful not to waste it. You do what's important to you and you spend time with people you care about.

❖ You give more thought to your decisions and actions because you know there may not be enough time to revise or undo them.

❖ You are less interested in material possessions than when you were younger. You get more pleasure out of a new friend or a new accomplishment than a new car.

❖ You take responsibility for yourself and stop blaming others for whatever has gone wrong in your life.

❖ You become more patient with the people in your life and don't require them to live up to all your expectations.

❖ You find ways to balance work, family, and friends.

❖ You realize you have your limitations, and you don't push yourself too hard.

❖ You learn to control your temper and, whenever possible, to use humor and empathy instead of anger in dealing with tense situations.

❖ You make it a top priority to keep your mind active and your body in good health.

❖ You're more comfortable with yourself than you would have thought possible when you were young.

❖ You enjoy your grown children, take pleasure in their independence, and do not try to influence or control them.

❖ You feel that you can still change your world instead of having to adapt to it.

❖ You keep an open mind and a flexible attitude toward the world around you so that you do not develop a narrow, rigid mindset.

❖ You stop playing games with time because you know that in the long run, time will win. You come to terms with the reality that, no matter how much plastic surgery you have, you cannot stop the aging process. Instead, you accept it with courage and good humor.

❖ You discover that, for every ending, there can be a new beginning.

MAKING THE TRANSITION

Middle age is very much a part of our contemporary consciousness, of our effort to break free from youth worship and confront the realities of the changing experience of aging in a longer-living society. Today, we think of aging in terms of transitions or passages rather than ages or stages. It is a more fluid perception of aging, one which envisions a process that is like a smooth flow of change rather than a bumpy journey over rigidly defined age boundaries.

The lives of today's middle-aged women have been marked by the shift in values of the '60s. This generation, more than any other in our history, has been faced with the challenge of living, as one family therapist describes the problem, "on two tracks simultaneously. They are pulled in two different directions and are looking for ways to become one-track women."

How can women cope with life on two tracks running in different directions? One solution would seem to be to discard the past and live strictly by the code of values and behavior of today. Why cling to the outmoded ideas that we were indoctrinated with before the women's movement and the sexual revolution? Why not leave all that behind us and fit in with the changing scene? Adaptation is the law of life, right?

But it is not so simple to tear out of our hearts and minds the values we absorbed in our formative years. Those of us who grew up in traditional families are warmed by memories of the closeness, the strength, the security of those family ties. We remember neighborliness, lifelong friendships, the feeling of belonging, and we are not ready to give up those values totally for the individualism, mobility, and rootlessness that characterize so much of life today.

But we also want to enjoy the new opportunities that have become available to us in recent years. We want our careers, our independence, our pride of achievement, and we also want children, a home, and someone to love and share it with. We want the freedom to be who we are, to live and love without the repressiveness that we have gladly left behind us, but we also want healthy, satisfying sexual relationships that are more than one-night stands.

Can we have it all? Or are we expecting too much? A recent Gallup poll revealed that 83 percent of women of childbearing age are confident that they can achieve their goals of marriage, children, and advancement in their careers. And they can find reassurance in the experience of midlife women who are demonstrating that having it all actually means fulfilling one's potential, which every one of us has a right to and which women today, whatever their age, have the opportunity and the means to achieve.

The lives of women in midlife are being energized by the new perception of middle age. Today the passage between youth and old age is seen as a time of change and growth, of self-assessment and self-affirmation, of a search for purpose and identity. It is a time of crisis and conflict but also of challenge and opportunity, a time to free the hidden self and make the most of one's newly discovered resources. For women in midlife, it is time for a well-earned celebration, a time to enjoy a new freedom and to realize long-deferred dreams.

BIBLIOGRAPHY

Badinter, Elisabeth, *The Myth of Motherhood*, Souvenir Press, Ltd., London, 1981

Baruch, Grace, and Brooks-Gunn, Jeanne, eds., *Women in Midlife*, Plenum Press, New York, 1984

Belsky, Janet, *Here Tomorrow*, The Johns Hopkins University Press, Baltimore, MD, 1988

Boston Women's Health Collective, *Our Bodies, Ourselves*, Simon and Schuster, New York, 1979

De Beauvoir, Simone, *The Coming of Age*, Warner Books, New York, 1975

Fried, Barbara, *The Middle-Age Crisis*, Harper and Row, New York, 1976

Lessing, Doris, *The Summer Before the Dark*, Bantam Books, New York, 1974

London, Mel, *Second Spring*, Rodale Press, Emmaus, PA, 1982

Melamed, Elissa, *Mirror, Mirror*, Linden Press/Simon and Schuster, New York, 1983

Tyler, Anne, *Breathing Lessons*, Alfred A. Knopf, New York, 1988

Wolf, Naomi, *The Beauty Myth*, William Morrow, New York, 1991

Wolfe, Sidney M., M.D., and Donkin-Jones, Rhoda, *Women's Health Alert*, Addison-Wesley, Reading, MA, 1990

INDEX

ABOUT THE AUTHOR

❧

Elinor Lenz is an author, teacher, and consultant in adult education. She has a master of arts from UCLA and teaches in the UCLA Extension Writing Program.

She serves as a consultant to various educational and media organizations and is frequently invited to lecture on the subjects of her books at professional conferences and community organizations.

Her books include:

❖ *So You Want to Go Back to School* (coauthor)

❖ *Once My Child, Now My Friend*

❖ *Effectiveness Training for Women* (coauthor)

❖ *The Feminization of America* (coauthor)

She has written for television and film and writes occasional book reviews for the *New York Times* and the *Los Angeles Times*. An essay, "The Generation Gap: From Persephone to Portnoy," was published in the *New York Times Book Review*.

❧